COUNSELOR TO COUNSELOR *July 23, 1975*

DATE DUE

GAYLORD 234			PRINTED IN U. S. A.

Counselor To Counselor

by

Lionel T. Campbell

Logos International
Plainfield, New Jersey

Library of Congress Catalog Card Number: 73-161423
Logos International, Plainfield, N.J. 07060

Printed in the United States of America

Dedication

"To those born-again believers throughout the world who by the dynamic power and leading and guidance of the Holy Spirit, The Counselor, are now: (1) revealing Jesus Christ as the Light and Answer to a darkened world and (2) edifying, strengthening and building up the Body of Christ, the true Church, in preparation for His soon coming."

ACKNOWLEDGMENTS

Grateful acknowledgment is made to the following for the use of copyright material:

Christian Life Magazine
Portions of chapter IV appeared originally in "A Lawyer Looks at the Gifts of the Spirit," © July 1965, Christian Life Publications, Inc., Gundersen Drive and Schmale Road, Wheaton, Illinois, 60187. Used by permission.

Logos Magazine
Material in chapter III draws heavily upon "The Power of Pentecost," by Thomas N. Foster, © August, November 1966, *Logos Magazine,* Christchurch, New Zealand. Used by permission.

Christ for the Nations
Material about the Welsh revival (chapter III) taken from "Oh the Wonder of It All," by Kay Pernia, © June 1968, Christ for the Nations, Dallas, Texas, 75216. Used by permission.

Beyond Ourselves
Some of the material and all the quotations under the sub-heading "You Must Know the Holy Spirit" in Chapter I are taken from the book *Beyond Ourselves* by Catherine Marshall © 1961, McGraw-Hill Book Company, New York, New York, 10036. Used by permission.

Chapter I

WITHOUT EXCUSE

A practicing attorney who fails to read the record, consider the testimony, weigh the evidence, and acquaint himself fully with the law in his search for the truth in any case which he is handling is, to put it mildly, foolish. If he himself is the defendant and his own life and liberty are at stake, he is more than foolish. If, in addition, he stubbornly refuses to meet and cooperate with counsel—well, he doesn't even have a prayer!

Yet I, a practicing lawyer, had for over twenty years failed to look at the Bible record or acquaint myself with God's eternal law. The record was there—an open Book available to me. It was I, and I alone, who was carelessly gambling with my own eternal soul in my life and death case before that court of last resort from which there can be no appeal and from whose final sentence there is neither reprieve nor parole!

Like any other lawyer I had practically cut my teeth on the truism that "ignorance of the law is no defense." Yet I was ignorant of the fact plainly written in the lexicon of God's law, the Bible: "You *must* be born again." The Book lay in my library unopened for two decades except perhaps for a desultory glance now and then to try to find an acceptable Scripture to support an argument to the jury. Here my ignorance became hypocrisy!

I was ignorant of all but the barest biblical facts concerning my own situation. Nor was I fully aware of the character and seriousness of the charges leveled against me in the Bible or of the penalty for guilt. I did not know the Bible states plainly we have made God a liar if we disbelieve the evidence, the record, and the testimony that God the Father has given regarding His Son, Jesus Christ (I John 5:9-11). What an awesome thought!

While I was not actively persecuting Christ and His Church, as was Saul of Tarsus at the time he traveled down the Damascus road, I was, by neglect and ignorance, guilty of failing to meet and to know Jesus Christ. I had always believed in God, but the realization of Jesus Christ as His Son and my personal Savior had never penetrated my consciousness.

God's Word plainly tells us that Jesus is "the way, the truth and the life," and that "no man comes to the Father except by Him." But I had never read the "transcript" of the Bible testimony regarding Him. Instead, I had, in a careless, slipshod fashion, relied only upon hearsay evidence! Nor had I even bothered to read the Bible record of that heavenly court in which Jesus Christ is named as *my* attorney—*my* Advocate and Mediator. I had not realized that for years He had been pleading my cause before the throne and in my behalf withstanding Satan, the "accuser of the brethren," who was producing abundant evidence against me and demanding the death penalty for my eternal soul!

In the life of each one of us there are great turning points which come in the form of experiences and events that shape our destinies. The major turning point in my life came in 1963, for in that year my beloved wife died, and I wept my way through the valley of bereavement. There, where the shadows were deep and it seemed no sunlight would ever again filter through, I found my Lord and Savior Jesus Christ.

During the bewilderment and confusion of those grievous months the realization dawned upon me that God knew—I knew—that I was guilty of sin! I took the only possible course—pleaded guilty, threw myself upon the mercy of the court, and asked for pardon. God graciously said: "Your sins are forgiven! Go, and sin no more."

INTELLECTUAL CHRISTIANITY

I was raised in a church-oriented home with regular Sunday school and other church attendance, accompanied by the usual denominational and doctrinal training. But no one ever explained to me, as Jesus explained to a sincere religious leader of His day named Nicodemus, that "except a man be *born again* (from above), he cannot see or enter the Kingdom of God" (John 3:3-5). Like Nicodemus, I was one who did not know the meaning of the words "born again." I was one of those nominal Christians who preferred an intellectual acceptance of Jesus Christ. I knew *of* Him, as the great teacher and prophet who somehow vaguely was the Son of God, but I did not know Him *in my heart.* I did not really know that He was the only begotten Son of God, born of a virgin—*God* in human flesh—who shed His blood for me that I might have God's own eternal life through Him.

By worldly standards, I had achieved some measure of accomplishment. I had been president of the student body at the University and graduated Phi Beta Kappa. After army duty in World War II, I had developed a successful law practice and had a beautiful wife, family and home. I was enjoying political, social, and bar association prestige; plus all the earthly possessions that mere money can buy. There was a certain limelight in all this, but I was without Jesus Christ, the true Light of the world, and had little knowledge of the Word of God (John 1:1-8). Later I was to learn the spiritual law that worldly limelight tends to kill and destroy, while the true Light always produces *life*—life not only more abundantly here and now, but life that is eternal.

A PERSONAL HEART ENCOUNTER

Without even realizing it, I had for years been spiritually blind—walking in spiritual darkness down that road which leads to eternal death and damnation. Although I *thought* I knew God, I had never experienced a personal heart encounter with the Lord Jesus Christ. I was not aware that Jesus said He is the *way,* the *truth,* and the *life* and that no man can come to the Father except by Him (John 14:6). I did not know that the Word of God further says that no man can say he knows God, the Father, unless he acknowledges Jesus Christ as the only begotten Son of the Father and as personal Savior and Lord of his life. As one translator has put it, "The man who will not recognize the Son cannot possibly know the Father" (I John 2:23, Phillips).

I tremble to think how many well-intentioned, respectable, likable, and successful people there are in America who are but nominal, social, intellectual, Sunday Christians. Their names are written on the church membership rolls but have never been written in God's Book of Life (Luke 10:20; Phil. 4:3). They have never been born again, have never personally met Jesus Christ and let Him come into their hearts. They are, as I was, walking in darkness and ignorance, sitting in the shadow of death (Luke 1:79), and do not even know it because no one has told them. From my observation there must be hundreds of thousands. I say this because I have asked many denominational people if they are "born again" only to receive a blank stare or to be asked what I meant by "born again."

For these people I have a loving burden because of my own former blindness. And it is especially for such that I offer this testimony of the saving power of the Gospel of Jesus Christ. But it is not *only* for them that this testimony is written. It is also to the truly born-again Christians of all denominations, who have indeed accepted Jesus into their hearts, but have not sought or received the same fullness, the same fire, and the same power that descended from heaven on the 120 at Pentecost 1900 years ago. This is the wondrous "second gift" of God to believers, for Jesus Christ is not only the Savior but also the mighty Baptizer!

WHAT I HAVE SEEN AND HEARD

Mine is *not* hearsay testimony!

Like Peter and John when they were confronted by the high priests and the Sadducees for speaking and teaching in the name of Jesus, *I cannot help speaking about what I have actually seen and heard* (Acts 4:20). Be assured that it is only by the power and authority and boldness of the blessed Holy Spirit that I am able to report to you these astonishing and marvelous truths. Although I earn my living with words, of myself I would stumble for want of adequate vocabulary to describe my experiences. However, I have joyously learned that although we can do nothing without Him, through Christ, who strengthens us, we can do all things (Phil. 4:13). My testimony is of the love, wisdom, and power of God, expressed and revealed through Jesus Christ our Lord by the Holy Spirit.

THE BILLY GRAHAM CRUSADE

During that awful six months after my first wife's death, with all the accompanying anguish, bewilderment, and searching, I and my children—two grown daughters and one son in high school—were suddenly confronted with a desperate need for more light on the truth. Reason and logic, the only pathway to truth that I knew, just wasn't answering the need, and I couldn't help the children who now looked to me for comfort.

Friends who had known my wife as a spiritual person who loved the Lord tried to assure us by saying that "God had taken her home." Home? Where? How? Legal training and my hit-and-miss church experience had not prepared me for this.

It was then that God moved. Through the prayers of many believers, some of whom we did not even know, my entire family was drawn to the Billy Graham Crusade at the Los Angeles Coliseum in September of 1963. The children, with their young minds uncluttered and unfettered by the ingrained laws of logic and argument which hindered me, seemed to glimpse the light at the other end of the dark tunnel before I did, and they urged that we attend more of the coliseum meetings.

Each meeting seemed to melt away more and more of the hard exterior of my heart, and finally, on the last night of the crusade, as Dr. Graham preached the Word—the *Good News* of salvation—the Holy Spirit suddenly broke through to my spiritual understanding. I realized God's marvelous plan of redemption through the shed blood of Jesus Christ. There were no oratorical pyrotechnics or extreme emotional urging, just the simple, logical presentation of free salvation available to all through a Savior whose love for all mankind was so great He was willing to die in our stead. Jesus had "taken the rap" for us, that we might not suffer the wages of sin which is death, but might inherit eternal life.

I had heard sermons before—heard them with my ears or my intellect—*but this one I heard with my heart.* When the invitation was given, a power not my own literally drew me out of my seat. I stood up, admitted I was a sinner, asked and received pardon, and publicly in the presence of 134,000 people confessed Jesus Christ as my Savior.

From that moment life has never been the same. Something very wonderful happened within my logical, literal soul. I saw and sensed old things passing away and all things becoming new. The world looked different. My love for my family was intensified. This was, of course, a fulfillment of II Cor. 5:17—a Scripture of which I was unaware until I began to read and joyously devour the Word of God. It says: "If any man be in Christ, he is a new creature: old things are passed away; behold all things are become new."

Among the things that began to pass away were unclean and lustful thoughts and actions, social drinking, impatience, telling off-color jokes or stories, and self-deceit. Among things that became new were: (1) a realization of being cleansed completely by the blood of Jesus Christ and the water of the Holy Word of God; (2) a desire to witness to the saving knowledge of Jesus Christ; (3) a desire to pray and praise the Lord; (4) a thirst and hunger for the Word of God; (5) a love of God and my fellowman; (6) a whole new family of Christian friends with whom to fellowship; and (7) a joy unspeakable at knowing Jesus Christ as my personal, risen and living Lord.

YOU MUST KNOW
THE HOLY SPIRIT

I did not know anything of the Person or administration of the Holy Spirit, or Holy Ghost, mentioned so prominently throughout the New Testament. The two names are of course synonymous, being identical in the Greek. Though now so real and blessed, the Holy Spirit was then an ethereal, vague, hazy, abstract, far-off, even "spooky" conception. I thought He was a "something," or an "it" floating around in space to which preachers and some other religious people occasionally tried to attach to prove some theological doctrine or support some ecclesiastical ritual. In all my church attendance no one had ever explained to me what or who the Holy Spirit is. How ignorant and uninformed I was!

In this connection it was of great interest to me to learn recently that Catherine Marshall LeSourd, widow of the late Peter Marshall and author of the best-selling books, *A Man Called Peter* and *Mr. Jones, Meet the Master,* had had a quite similar understanding or lack of understanding of the Holy Spirit before she came to know Him (as I also came to know Him) through the baptism in the Holy Spirit. In her book entitled *Beyond Ourselves* she tells how she came to know the Holy Spirit. A few short quotations and references will illustrate the similarity between our concepts of the Holy Spirit before and after meeting Him.

"Like most people," she says, "I had thought of the Holy Spirit as a theological abstraction, a sort of ecclesiastical garnish for christenings, weddings, benedictions and the like. As for the term, *the Holy Ghost,* that I regarded as archaic, if not downright eerie." [1] A friend told her of having received an experience of the baptism in the Holy Spirit. Mrs. LeSourd tells of replying to her friend's story by admitting that the Holy Spirit had an insignificant and unnecessary place in her life, and of saying, "He's nothing to me. I've had no contact with Him and could get along quite well without Him." [2]

Later, from a study of the Bible with her concordance, she discovered her misconception. She states that she found out that He was a person, not an "influence" or "a thing," but in a sense "He is both the most basic and most modest member of the Trinity, for His work is to reflect Christ and to glorify Him." [3]

She further writes that we need, "the Holy Spirit to make Christ's glory perceptible to us. It is as if the Holy Spirit gives us a new way of seeing, with which we can perceive spiritual

[1] Catherine Marshall, *Beyond Ourselves* (New York: McGraw-Hill Book Company 1961; Spire Books, 1970), p. 231.

[2] *Ibid.,* p. 233.

[3] *Loc. cit.*

truth where all has been darkness before . . . "[4]

She discovered further that "there is nothing ethereal, no trace of the sanctimonious humbug that most people expect to find in the Holy Spirit. Nor is there any saccharine sentimentality. Quite the contrary; there is a down-to-earth quality of personality about the Holy Spirit so marked that I still would not believe it had I not experienced it."[5]

Without reservation I concur and agree through my own personal experience with all of the delightful discoveries made by Mrs. LeSourd about the person, nature, and work of the blessed Holy Spirit.

It is now difficult, however, to believe that I once was walking in such colossal ignorance about such eternal matters. From my experience, the experience of Mrs. LeSourd and others, it is safe to say that regrettably there must be literally hundreds of thousands, perhaps millions, of members of historic Christian churches today who still do not know the Holy Spirit and who view Him in the same misconceived and misunderstood dimension as Mrs. LeSourd and I did before we received the baptism in the Holy Spirit. I pray that the admission and exposure of my own ignorance will lead those who do not really know Him to re-examine the Scriptures and their own concept or lack of concept of the Holy Spirit. To them, from a deep and loving burden in my heart, may I say that if you want to know more about the person and the nature of the Father and of His son and our Lord, Jesus Christ, and His love, power and wisdom in your daily life, seek and receive the baptism in the Holy Spirit and come to know the third person of the Godhead who is the agent and the messenger who reveals Jesus Christ to us in all His fullness and glory.

How the cares, attractions and pressures of the complex world in which we live, coupled with my neglect of the things of God and eternity, had kept me in ignorance—not only of the things of Christ, but also of the Holy Spirit to whom God has given the ministry of revealing Christ in us in all His fullness (John 14:16-17, 26; 15:26; 16:7-15). Indeed He is

[4]*Ibid.*, p. 234.
[5]*Ibid.*, p. 237.

referred to by Jesus as the "Spirit of Truth" who will guide us into all truth (John 16:13). Thus, by a magnificent spiritual formula of God—as certain and sure as any natural mathematical equation—the Holy Spirit of Truth *always* witnesses and leads us to Jesus Christ who *is* the Truth. He *always* shows us the way to Jesus Christ who *is* the Way. He *always* brings us to life in Jesus Christ who *is* the Life (John 14:6).

To me, the startling fact was that my deliverance from the power and dominion of darkness into the marvelous light and Kingdom of the Son of God was in complete accord with the Scriptures *with which I was then unfamiliar.* I hadn't read, nor had I been instructed as to what God's Word said would occur upon adoption into the family of God (Rom. 8:14-17). I experienced these things *before* I read about them. I had to read and be instructed later in order to fully understand what had happened to me! The following account is what happened—simply what I *saw* and *felt* and *heard*—within the next few days after my Savior found me.

BAPTISM IN THE HOLY SPIRIT

The next morning after that last momentous meeting at the coliseum I was awakened early. An overwhelming power struck me like a bolt out of heaven, as if a great seal had been stamped on the side of my body. Suddenly there was a warm, glowing, all-encompassing power gushing and flowing back and forth, up and down from the crown of my head to the soles of my feet, like liquid electricity. Flowing waves of glory engulfed me. It seemed as if Someone was there fanning the flow back and forth.

Accompanying this phenomenon was such a love of God pouring into and out of my heart through my lips that I could not contain it. A tremendous surge of joy filled my soul. It seemed I should die from sheer inability to contain this overwhelming ocean of love—I felt that it would surely break me to pieces if I could not somehow release it. Indeed, this was evidently the beginning of the breaking of my old nature, accompanied by my birth as a new creature in Christ Jesus (II Cor. 5:17). During this experience, it seemed that I was lifted up, whether in the body or in the spirit I don't know, and shown that God is Love and that *the eternal ultimate of all man's striving, existence, and purpose is to come into the full knowledge and possession of this love of God which has been placed in Christ Jesus for us.*

I began to release this love in prayer for others, which prayers God later answered in miraculous ways, even including physical healings. Also, within me was suddenly born an overwhelming hunger and thirst to read the Word of God, accompanied by an irresistible desire to tell others of the love of Jesus Christ. An equally deep desire sprang up to praise God and to thank and acknowledge Him in every facet of my life. This latter desire was in part a manifestation and fulfillment, by the indwelling power of the Holy Spirit, of the Word of God set forth in I Thess. 5:18, Col. 3:17, and Eph. 5:20.

These three Scripture verses enjoin us to give thanks unto God the Father for and in all things in the name of our Lord Jesus Christ. But they were totally unknown to me at the time the Holy Spirit put them into my heart with the desire and power to obey and give effect to them. Later, of course, I read these verses in the Bible. What a delight it was to discover that the Holy Spirit had taught my heart a portion of God's Word without my mind and intellect first reading it in print and trying to debate or reason it out in the natural! What a Teacher we have in the blessed Holy Spirit! (I John 2:27). He first got hold of this lawyer's *heart*—without any argument or debate—placing therein eternal truths that the lawyer's *head* later confirmed in the written Word of God.

Immediately following my conversion my heart was so filled with love for my Lord it was impossible to find enough English words to adequately express all the love and praise that welled up within me. I was repeating myself—using the same words over and over again in my prayers—until it became embarrassing to me. Here I was, a lawyer, making a living by words—a wordsmith so to speak—yet unable to find a sufficient number and variety of English words to express the love, joy and thanksgiving for our salvation and for all of the Lord's blessings and answers to prayer that my soul felt and that I was aching to release.

Now, at that time I knew nothing, absolutely nothing,

about the meaning of Pentecost. I didn't even know what the word meant (except the prefix "pente" meant 50th of something), much less that it was spoken of prominently in the 2nd Chapter of the Book of Acts. I had never read the Book of Acts, nor recollect having ever heard any minister preach or quote therefrom. I did not know what the nine gifts of the Spirit were as set forth by the Apostle Paul in I Corinthians, Chapter 12. Nor did I have any understanding of the nine characteristics of the fruit of the Spirit enumerated in Galatians 5:22. I was unaware that at the time of Pentecost, A.D. 33, the disciples had been filled with the Holy Spirit and had spoken with other languages as the Spirit gave utterance (Acts, Chapt. 2). I didn't know that anyone had ever then or since spoken in other tongues they had not learned. Nor had I ever heard anyone speak in languages or tongues unknown to the speaker. In short, here again I was plainly ignorant and uninformed of the existence of one of God's most precious gifts for born-again believers. Nevertheless it is all plainly revealed in the Scriptures for all to read, see, seek, receive and use for His glory!

When I complained to the Lord about running out of English words with which to pray, worship, and praise Him, I did not ask to speak in other tongues, because I knew nothing of tongues. But the Lord Jesus Christ, who is the mighty Baptizer (Matt. 3:11; Luke 3:16 and 24:49; John 1:33; Acts 1:5 and 2:33), saw my need and heard the cry of my heart. As He always does, when our requests are made in love, obedience, faith, and in accordance with His will and for His glory, the Lord answered my need—in a most unexpected and startling way. Several days later, early in the morning I awoke and began my morning prayers, apologizing to the Lord for being repetitious because of my poverty of words. Suddenly this same flowing power, which had filled my whole being a few days earlier (and Who, praise God, has remained with me as promised in John 14:16), again surged up like springs or rivers of living water (John 7:38) from my innermost being to the area of my throat. Spontaneously I began to pour forth a gushing flow of beautiful tongues and languages! It was as if Someone from the depths of my soul, bypassing my material mind, was using my organs of speech, vocal chords, tongue and lips. In short, I was supplying and using these physical organs and speaking, but the words were not mine nor were they formed by my intellect!

[May I interject here that I did not then know that in about A.D. 60, the Holy Spirit speaking through the Apostle James had said that no man can tame the tongue because it is an unruly member, a poison, a world of iniquity, and a flame of destructive fire if not disciplined and controlled (James 3:5-10). But I soon learned that when we surrender it in obedience to God, He can tame it and use it for His glory. In fact, the Scriptures tell us that the baptism in the Holy Spirit is also a baptism of fire (Matt. 3:11; Luke 3:16; 12:49-50). Our tongues then become on fire for God to carry out His holy will and purposes, for He makes His ministers a flaming fire! (Ps. 104:4).]

It was most startling and astonishing! Yet my mind, my intellect, and my awareness of what was happening were all operating normally and clearly. Since the words were not mine, I sensed this was of God because it was so full of glory. I also sensed that there was a great pouring out of praise to God. But the question kept recurring in my mind: "What does this all mean?" (Later I discovered to my amazement that my question was quite scriptural. In Acts 2:1-12 we read that devout men then residing in Jerusalem from every nation, who heard at Pentecost the 120 speaking in other tongues, including in each of their own dialects or languages, were amazed and said: "What can this mean?")

The tongues seemed to change from time to time as if from glory to glory. Some sounded Arabic, some a soft Polynesian, some Oriental, some Greek, some Italian, some of a guttural nature, but none was identifiable by me. I had never studied, learned, or spoken any foreign language except Spanish, and I did not recognize any Spanish.

This outpouring of praise and glory to God continued for about one hour without ceasing. I had no power, nor did I desire it, to stop. Most of the outpouring was heard and witnessed by my three children who were awakened and came to my bedroom. This was the first time any of the four of us had ever heard speaking in other tongues! How unsearchable are the wonders of God and His ways beyond finding out! It is not surprising that the Psalmist was prompted to cry out, "your knowledge is too wonderful for me. It is high above me" (Ps. 139:6).

THE DODGER PROPHECY

Suddenly the tongues ceased, and immediately something equally astounding occurred. I spoke out in perfect English, with no knowledge of what was coming forth, prophetic words as follows: "Ballplayer, ballplayer, ballplayer! Skowron is a man touched by God. He will be one of the heroes of the World Series. The Dodgers will win the pennant. The Dodgers will win the World Series. New York will lose. New York will lose. New York will lose!"

This occurred in September, 1963, before the Los Angeles team had even won the National League pennant, much less the World Series against the New York Yankees who were long-odds favorites that year. In the natural, this prophecy sounded impossible of fulfillment. But God, who knows the past, present, and future, the beginning and the end of all things (Jesus Christ is the Alpha and the Omega) knew ahead of time exactly the outcome of these events. This type of prophecy was, of course, described by Peter at the time of Pentecost (over 1900 years ago) as a fulfillment of that which was spoken by the prophet Joel (800 years before Pentecost): "And it shall come to pass in the last days, saith God, I will pour out of my Spirit upon all flesh; and your sons and daughters shall prophesy . . . (Acts 2:16-17).

At first, in the natural, I did not understand why God had used a baseball player and a baseball team as the subject matter of a prophecy. As I later searched the Scriptures, however, I discovered God frequently used events and things commonly known to the people concerned to illustrate His Word demonstrate His eternal power and purpose (Matt. 6:28-29; 13:47-48; 20:1-16). I am now persuaded that this message was given to me for a threefold purpose.

First, it was a demonstration to me of the depth of the magnificent power, wisdom, and knowledge of God which is placed in Jesus Christ for us (I Cor. 1:24, 30; Col. 1:19; 2:9-10; Rom. 11:33).

Secondly, I was enabled thereby, through a series of very

exceptional circumstances, to witness to Walter Alston, the Dodgers' manager, of the saving knowledge and power of the Gospel of Jesus Christ. This was after the World Series had been won by the Dodgers, almost unbelievably and without precedent, in four straight games. Alston conceded that some strange and unaccountable things had happened in the World Series. He had not yet figured out just how or why his team had won the last two games. I remarked that I did not know why either, but I felt God was surely trying to show us something. He said he thought God was too busy to be concerned with such things as ball games and baseball players.

"Not so," I said, "because our God knows such small things as the fall of every sparrow and even the number of hairs on our heads. He is interested in and knows all things and all people whomsoever, ballplayers included." And I added that it was evident from the prophecy that God had become concerned in the affairs of the Dodger team generally and Bill Skowron particularly. (Later, I discovered that while I was witnessing to Mr. Alston, the Holy Spirit had brought Scriptures to me that I had no recollection of ever having read).

In fact, it developed that Mr. Alston had not definitely decided to play Skowron in the World Series until a day or so before the first game, because Skowron had had one of the worst seasons in his career. From the prophecy it became clearly evident to us that God knew at least three weeks before Alston knew that Skowron was going to play in the World Series and would be one of the heroes—which indeed he was!

Thirdly, the Lord opened the door for me to give a brief witness for Christ to Bill Skowron on the telephone before he left Los Angeles. A few months later I was led of the Spirit to mail to each member of the team a copy of *Voice* magazine, containing the stirring testimony of baseball pitcher Al Worthington who had also found Jesus Christ as Savior and Lord at a Billy Graham Crusade in San Francisco under circumstances somewhat parallel to mine.

None of the above events was the result of any power or cleverness on my part, but all were done in the power and by the direction of the Holy Spirit. I am believing and praying that as many other players as the Lord our God will call will come to Christ by the subsequent watering by other Christians of this and other implanted seeds of the Word, which God will cause to grow and mature into salvation (I Cor. 3:6-9).

When we begin to see the fantastic manifestations of the power and purpose of God around us, we begin to understand why the apostle Paul cried out, "Oh, the depths of the riches both of the wisdom and knowledge of God!" (Rom. 11:33).

SEEKING MORE LIGHT

The morning I received the gift of other languages, another strange set of circumstances occurred. The telephone rang. It was Tim Sims, a family friend who was working for George Stevens, the director of the motion picture, *The Greatest Story Ever Told* at Metro-Goldwyn-Mayer Studio in Culver City, California. He reported that Billy Graham would be at MGM later that morning for about an hour to make some shots for a television film spectacular on the life of Cecil B. DeMille. Knowing that our whole family had just been converted at the Graham Crusade, Ted suggested that we come to the studio that morning and meet Dr. Graham personally.

Still practically walking on air after my tremendous experience with the Lord, I was delighted at the possibility of discussing it with Dr. Graham. I was eagerly seeking for the scriptural explanation of what had happened to me, and was most happy for an opportunity to discuss it with such a man of God. It seemed that here was God's answer to my prayer for guidance, particularly inasmuch as outsiders are seldom admitted during such audio filmings, and our invitation was almost a miracle in itself.

Two hours after canceling all office appointments, I, our good friend Tim, and Sandra and Pat, my two daughters, were introduced to Dr. Graham at the studio. Between "takes" he graciously sat down with us in an enclosed makeup room on the set.

Ordinarily I am a calm, logical individual. But perhaps my demeanor that morning, as I tried to describe the events of the past few days and particularly of the last few hours, was a bit over-exuberant. It is not an ordinary thing to be confronted by a trial attorney with a rehearsal of such an unusual and supernatural set of events. Undoubtedly the same joy the 120 radiated at Pentecost still expressed itself in my actions. In a spiritual sense, I *was* full of the fresh new wine of the Holy Spirit (Acts 2:15-17). All that had happened to me had been in a spirit filled with the love and praise of God and great joy, peace, and trust in Jesus Christ. I asked Dr. Graham the question recorded in Acts 2: "What does this mean?"

Doctor Graham replied by indicating that he was interested because he had a friend who had recently come into this same experience of speaking in tongues.

At this point we were interrupted by a call for Dr. Graham to return to the video cameras again.[6] However, he sent Grady Wilson, one of his team associates, to talk with us. Mr. Wilson came over and sat down, opened a copy of the New Testament and expounded to us the Scriptures on the baptism in the Holy Spirit, the gift of tongues, the spiritual gifts and fruit of the Spirit. He read and explained parts of the Gospel of St. John, I Cor. 12, 13, and 14, and also Acts 1 and 2. He pointed out, and I read *for the first time,* Peter's immortal and amazing answer to the devout men in Jerusalem who first heard the 120 speak in tongues:

14 But Peter, standing up with the eleven, lifted up his voice, and said unto them, Ye men of Judea, and all ye that dwell at Jerusalem, be this known unto you, and hearken to my words;

15 For these are not drunk, as ye suppose, seeing it is but the third hour of the day.

16 But this is that which was spoken through the prophet, Joel:

[6] Later I learned that Mr. Graham's interest in the gifts, baptism, and work of the Holy Spirit had had earlier and broader implications. As reported in the January 1961 issue of the Full Gospel Business Men's magazine, *Voice,* Dr. Graham, in addressing a ministers' group in Sacramento, California, commented: "In the main denominations we have looked a bit askance at our brethren from the Pentecostal churches because of their emphasis on the doctrine of the Holy Spirit, *but I believe the time has come to give the Holy Spirit His rightful place in our churches. We need to learn once again what it means to be baptized with the Holy Spirit."*

17 And it shall come to pass in the last days, saith God, I will pour out of my Spirit upon all flesh, and your sons and your daughters shall prophesy, and your young men shall see visions, and your old men shall dream dreams;

18 And on my servants and on my handmaidens I will pour out in those days of my Spirit, and they shall prophesy:

19 And I will show wonders in heaven above, and signs in the earth beneath: blood, and fire, and vapor of smoke.

20 The sun shall be turned into darkness, and the moon into blood, before that great and notable day of the Lord come;

21 And it shall come to pass that whosoever shall call on the name of the Lord shall be saved. (Acts 2:14-21. See also Matt. 3:11; Mark 1:8; 16:17; Luke 3:16; 11:13; 24:49; John 1:33; 7:37-39; 14:16, 26; 15:26; 16:7-15.)

From Mr. Wilson's expounding of the Scriptures I understood with awe and wonderment that this which had happened to me was that of which the prophet Joel had spoken and also that which had happened to the 120 at Pentecost (Acts 2: 1-20).

This was a most blessed time! It was the guidance for which my soul longed! It answered my immediate questions and pointed me to the Scripture passages for study and prayer for Holy Spirit enlightenment.

My very soul was thrilled at the account of Peter who, moved by the anointing of the selfsame Holy Spirit, stood up and gave that astounding, shattering, and world-shaking sermon and prophecy of what had happened and what would happen regarding Jesus Christ, the Son of God, whom they had crucified, and the great gift of the Holy Spirit which they had just *seen and heard* outpoured on the 120, that would be received upon repentance and acceptance of Jesus Christ by all believers throughout all generations—even down to this day! (Acts 2:33-41).

Within a period of three weeks, one daughter and my son were baptized in the Holy Spirit and spoke in other languages. Three months later, in Phoenix, Arizona, at a Full Gospel Businessmen's Fellowship meeting, several Spirit-filled Christian men and women laid hands on my other daughter and prayed with her. Suddenly she burst forth singing the music of the hymn "Oh, How I Love Jesus." The words, however, were not in English, but in another language or tongue! Someone present recognized this as a distinct, beautiful French dialect. My daughter had never studied, read, or spoken any French in her life!

SEARCH OF THE SCRIPTURES

Having been introduced to these Scriptures through Billy Graham and Grady Wilson, I began prayerfully to search into the ministry of the Holy Spirit. *This investigation was made without any preconceived doctrinal teaching, denominational creed, belief, or seminary training.* I was simply searching for the fullness of the truth as to what had happened to me and my family. It has proved to be the most continuously exciting and thrilling adventure of my life. It has become the unfolding of the dramatic walk in the Spirit, revealing the living reality of eternal life in the risen Christ. Equally amazing, the Guide and Teacher in this inquiry was, and continues to be, the blessed Holy Spirit Himself (John 14:26; 16:13).

I think of this experience as the training and teaching received by a young lawyer from head of the law firm. *It is like Counselor to Counselor.* Except here we are dealing with The Eternal Counselor, of the Head of the Universe, the Holy Spirit of eternal Truth, the Spirit of Christ Himself. How do we know this? The Scriptures tell us so.

One of the names given to Jesus Christ, as the coming Messiah, 740 years before His birth, is *Counselor:*

> "For unto us a child is born, unto us a son is given: and the government shall be on His shoulder: and His name shall be called Wonderful, *Counselor,* The Mighty God, The everlasting Father, The Prince of Peace." (Isa. 9:6) (Emphasis added)

Shortly before Jesus was arrested and taken before the high priest, He spoke to His disciples about some of the things that would happen after He went away. Most important was the fact that they would receive the Holy Spirit whom Jesus referred to as the Comforter or the *Counselor:*

"If you love me, you will keep my commandments. And I will pray the Father, and He will give you another *Counselor,* to be with you forever, even the Spirit of truth, whom the world cannot receive, because it neither sees Him nor knows Him; you know Him, for He dwells within you, and will be in you." (John 14:15, 16 Revised Standard Version) (Emphasis added)

"I have told you these things while I am still with you. But the Comforter *(Counselor,* Helper, Intercessor, Advocate, Strengthener, Standby), the Holy Spirit, whom the Father will send in My name (in My place, to represent Me and act on My behalf), He will teach you all things. And He will cause you to recall—will remind you of, bring to your remembrance—everything I have told you." (John 14:25, 26 Amplified Bible) (Emphasis added)

In II Corinthians 3:17 we read that the Lord is the Spirit and where the Spirit of the Lord is, there is liberty.

So I learned that the Holy Spirit is *The Counselor,* representing and acting on behalf of Jesus Christ, the Son, (as well as God the Father—the Three are one) here on earth. The same eternal truths that the disciples learned at the feet of Jesus in A.D. 33, the believers may learn today in faith through the Holy Spirit. And even more truths! (John 14:12; 21:25). Having once grasped this fantastic, yet simple, operation of God, I immediately "enrolled" in the School of the Holy Spirit—an earthly counselor seeking *The Heavenly Counselor.*

Chapter II

THE SCHOOL OF THE HOLY SPIRIT

It became clear to me, after reading John 14:26; 15:26 and 16:7-15, I John 2:27, and I Cor. 2:13, that the Holy Spirit is the One who, among other things, will testify, not of Himself but of Jesus, will guide us into *all truth,* show us *things to come,* and teach us *all things.* Then the Holy Spirit taught me from other Scriptures the truth of the union of Christ with the Father (John 17:21), the union of the believer with Christ, and the indwelling of Christ through the Holy Spirit in the believer (John 14:20). Next, after reading II Pet. 1:21 and II Tim. 3:16, I found that the Holy Spirit of God moved upon and inspired the writers of the Bible to record the Word of God, which is eternal truth, living and enduring forever (I Pet. 1:23).

Thus He is the writer, by inspiration of the minds and hands of men, of the Living Word from the heart and mouth of God the Father. So, too, I Cor. 2:10-14 told me that the Holy Spirit *knows and searches all things* that God has prepared for us, even the deep, profound, and unfathomable things of God, and reveals them to us. This means that the Holy Spirit is omniscient as well as omnipresent and omnipotent. Moreover, with the anointing of the Holy Spirit abiding in us we really don't need any other teacher, for He teaches us the truth and never a lie (I John 2:20-27).

What a teacher, indeed! What a magnificent and staggering realization that we can be taught by God Himself through the Holy Spirit, the third person of the Godhead! Like a child I believed what I read and concluded with certainty that only the Holy Spirit, [who Jesus said is the Spirit of Truth (John 14:17)], could lead, advise, help, teach, comfort, and guide me into *all* things, including above all the reality of the

Godhead. Who, then, would know more about the meaning of the baptism in the Holy Spirit, the gifts and the fruit of the Spirit, and the other marvelous revelations of Jesus than the Holy Spirit Himself? So in faith I put myself into His hands and entered His school, much of the time on my knees at my bedside. I expect to be in attendance at His blessed school the rest of my natural life, or until the Lord comes. Hallelujah!

The materials used in this holy school are: (1) the Bible, the inspired Word of God, as anointed and made alive by the Holy Spirit through prayerful and faithful study and reading; (2) the preaching, teaching, writing, and fellowship of Holy Spirit-anointed ministers and members of the Body of Christ;[1] and (3) the constant stream of new revelations of Christ Jesus brought by the Holy Spirit through the gifts and as the fruit of the Spirit—in short, the Living Word in action.

What I have learned in the past six years would fill several volumes. Even then I would scarcely have scratched the surface of the vast, immeasurable storehouse of the eternal knowledge and wisdom, learning and understanding placed in Christ Jesus for us through the Holy Spirit (I Cor. 1:24, 30; Col. 2:2-3). Among these, the Holy Spirit will show us the truth of things around, about, and in us, as seen from the worldly and temporal viewpoint. In the compass of this testimony I will try to highlight a few of these treasures of truth learned in the school of the Holy Spirit. Without a denominational tag, doctrine, creed, or dogma, and only in

[1] Among those whose preaching, teachings, writings, and fellowship the Holy Spirit has used for my schooling and growth in the knowledge, wisdom, and love of the Lord Jesus Christ and life in the Spirit are: Raymond Schoch, Pastor and Bible Teacher, Faith Center, Glendale, California, and KHOF and KHOF-TV, radio and television gospel outreaches of Faith Center; Dr. Willard C. Pierce, Dean of the Faith Center Bible School, California; David du Plessis, author of *The Spirit Bade Me Go* and authority on the Holy Spirit; Dr. Billy Graham, evangelist, and *Decision Magazine;* Robert Walker, editor of *Christian Life Magazine;* Oral Roberts, evangelist; Demos Shakarian, president of the F.G.B.M.F.I. and its fellowship; Tommy Tyson, Methodist evangelist; Dr. William Standish Reed, M.D., Episcopal surgeon and author; Dr. Robert Frost, biologist, lecturer, and author of *Aglow With the Spirit;* Rev. Dennis J. Bennett, Episcopal rector and author of *Nine O'clock in the Morning* of St. Luke's Church, Seattle, Washington; *Trinity Magazine;* the *Autobiography of Charles Finney;* Christian Business Men's Committee fellowship; Bob Mumford, Bible teacher, author of *15 Steps Out;* and hundreds of other dear members of the Body of Christ whose names, fellowship, and edification are not mentioned here simply for lack of space, but whose names are written in the Book of Life (Heb. 11:32; Phil. 4:3).

the love of Christ, I share what I have seen and heard in the hope and with the prayer that it will be both a blessing and challenge to His church today.

TWENTIETH CENTURY RENEWAL OF THE FIRST CENTURY CHURCH

There is an old song, "Pentecost is real, no matter what they say." This is the song that hundreds of thousands of denominational and nondenominational Christians across the United States and around the world are singing in their hearts today. Like the men at Ephesus and Samaria and the household of Cornelius, they have discovered that Pentecost is an experience of God, not a denomination of man, and that God, being no respecter of persons, is likewise no respecter of denominations when bestowing His gifts. They are discovering that Pentecost is God's answer to restore the church to her original purity and power. The Pentecostal outpouring of the baptism in the Holy Spirit has fallen on Episcopalians, Methodists, Baptists, Lutherans, and Presbyterians in great number and in lesser measure upon members of some 30 or more other denominations, representing a broad cross-section of American Protestantism, upon many born-again, nondenominational Christians, as well as more recently upon many Roman Catholics, including priests, nuns, and laymen. At one laymen's seminar on the Holy Spirit held on the campus of Oral Roberts University in Tulsa, Oklahoma, I met and fellowshiped with over 350 Christians from some 25 different denominational backgrounds who had received the Pentecostal experience of the baptism in the Holy Spirit. And what love, peace, and joy was expressed there in the bond and unity of the Spirit!

BOOK OF ACTS BECOMES ALIVE

Many of those who have received this blessing bear witness that the Book of Acts has suddenly become alive to them. It is no longer merely a history of the Apostolic church, but is the exciting, living Word of God account of the dynamic work of the blessed Holy Spirit in building and maintaining the Body of Christ today.

With the infilling, the truths of the Book of Acts are suddenly revealed to us by the Author, the Holy Spirit (Who moved upon the beloved physician St. Luke to put in writing the record of how the Church of Jesus Christ came into being and should normally function in the constant living flow of the miraculous). The normal Christian life begins to unfold before our spiritual eyes. We begin to see the power, authority, love, fire, and boldness that marks the walk of a believer baptized by immersion in the Holy Spirit. Suddenly we are with Peter and John at the gate called Beautiful. We are thrilled as we see and hear Peter command the lame man to rise and walk in Jesus' name. We see him healed, rising to his feet, leaping and walking and praising God! (Acts 3:1-10). We feel the vital reality of Tabitha being raised from the dead by the resurrection power of the Word of the Lord flowing through Peter by the Holy Spirit (Acts 9:40-41).

The Book of Acts has no "Amen" at the end, because it is an open-end record of the formation of the Body of Christ. It represents the original blueprint and pattern of the gifts and administrations of the Holy Spirit in this church age in the continuous revelation of Jesus Christ and the preparation of His Bride. It is a living, continuous, vital record of the Living Word in action. Through the centuries, countless thousands of additional chapters and verses have already been recorded here and in heaven. Thousands more are now daily being so recorded, and thousands more will be recorded in the future until our Lord, the Amen Himself (Rev. 3:14), returns for His Church, and writes "finished" to this particular record.

While there may be variations in sequence, manner, and timing, the same general pattern runs throughout the record given to us.

SALVATION—THE BORN-AGAIN EXPERIENCE

First, the sinner hears the Gospel, in faith believes in his heart on Jesus Christ, repents, confesses Jesus with his mouth and is born again by the will and Spirit of God (Acts 2:38; 8:13, 37; 16:31; 19:2; John 1:12-13; 3:5-6; Eph. 2:8; Rom. 10:9-10). The Holy Spirit sent of God the Father from above enters the sinner, quickens and makes alive his own spirit which had before been dead in trespasses and sins from the Adamic nature (Eph. 2:1, 5). In this operation he is sealed by the Holy Spirit in the measure of a down payment or earnest of the Spirit which is the pledge, guarantee, or foretaste of our inheritance (Eph. 1:13-14; II Cor. 5:5). But this work of the Holy Spirit in urging and leading us to salvation is not the baptism in or the overflowing of the Holy Spirit, although the two *may* occur almost simultaneously. When he is born again the regenerated one is "baptized" by the Holy Spirit into the Body of Christ and becomes a member of the Body. But this is only the beginning. There is more to come.

BAPTISM IN WATER

Second, he is then or later baptized in water as an outward evidence of inward repentance and as a symbol of his identification with the death, burial, and resurrection of our Lord Jesus (Acts 2:38; 8:16, 38-39; 10:47-48; 16:33; 19:3-5). However, in the sovereign will of God, the Holy Spirit may fall upon and completely immerse a person as he hears the Word and believes on Jesus, and before he is baptized in water. That is, he may be born again *of* or *by* (the agency of) the Holy Spirit sent of the Father, and immediately thereafter baptized in the Holy Spirit *by* (the agency of) Jesus Christ, the Son, who is *the* Baptizer. Thereafter, water baptism may follow. Such was the sequence—namely, (1) salvation, (2) baptism *in* the Holy Spirit with accompanying speaking in tongues, and (3) baptism in water—in the case of Cornelius, his relatives, and close friends (Acts 10:44-48).

The twelve disciples at Ephesus, however, were first baptized with John's baptism of repentance, that is, in water. Later, when Paul visited and found they did not know there was a Holy Spirit, they were rebaptized in water in the name of Jesus. Then Paul laid hands upon them, the Holy Spirit (sent by Jesus) came upon and immersed them, and they spoke with tongues and prophesied (Acts 19:1-7). This latter was obviously the baptism or immersion *in* the Holy Spirit spoken of by John the Baptist (Matt. 3:11; Mark 1:8; Luke 3:16; John 1:33) with speaking in tongues and prophesying as two of the outward manifestations (Acts 2:4, 17; Mark 16:17).

CHAPTER V

THE OTHER SIDE OF THE FENCE

I am especially partial to R.A. Torrey's emphasis, which is that the baptism of the Holy Spirit is for bringing men to Christ. In his book, *How To Bring Men To Christ,* he devotes an entire chapter to this most important thing. Torrey says:

"There is one condition of success in bringing men to Christ and that is of cardinal importance, and so little understood that it demands a separate chapter. I refer to the Baptism of the Holy Spirit. . . . What is the Baptism of the Holy Spirit? It is a definite and distinct operation of the Holy Spirit of which one may know whether it has been wrought in him or not. . . . The Baptism of the Holy Spirit always imparts power for service, the services to which God calls us. . . . This Baptism is an absolutely essential preparation for Christian work. . . . There must be definite prayer for this baptism. It is often said that the Holy Spirit is already here and that every believer has the Holy Spirit and so we ought not to pray for the Spirit. This argument overlooks the distinction between having the Holy Spirit and having this specific operation of the Holy Spirit. It also contradicts the plain teaching of God's Word that He gives 'the Holy Spirit to them that ask Him.' It is furthermore shown to be fallacious by the fact that the Baptism of the Holy Spirit in the book of Acts was constantly given in connection with and in answer to prayer." [1]

W.S. Boardman, another great stalwart of the faith, adds:

"The first great felt want that arises in the souls is that of deliverance from sin and temptation, met by the grace of God in Christ Jesus. The second great necessity as it arises is that of enduement, power is needed as well . . . enduement

[1] R.A. Torrey, *How to Bring Men to Christ* (Chicago: Revell, 1893), p. 104.

with resurrection life and power in Jesus by the Baptism of the Holy Spirit." [2]

What About Tongues?

Many people ask, "But what about speaking in tongues? What use is it? We don't need tongues anymore."

It would seem some people see no value whatever in gifts which they do not happen to have, whereas all the value is in those gifts which they possess. Regardless of what the scriptures actually say, some still wave aside these "temporary gifts" as of no value, no practical use for either Christian or the unsaved. Briefly, therefore, let us see what God in His Word has to say about just one of His Spirit's gifts, one of the most controversial and talked about—speaking in tongues.

What are tongues for? First I must state that I have never found a serious attempt by any dispensationalist to explain what tongues were for in the early church according to the Bible. If they don't believe it is for today's church, at least they might attempt to show why it was for the early church. But the books say nothing.

The Bible, however, says that the gift of tongues is for several purposes:

1. For personal, private prayer. I Cor. 14:2-4 says that the one who speaks in tongues edifies himself, for he speaks directly to God and not to other men. "Edify" means to "build up" or "improve." How does "speaking in tongues" build or edify? Those who have the gift testify that it is just that, a means of building their faith, enabling them to grow in Christ just as the scriptures promise. They also speak of it as a "release," a big help in their prayer life which is a fulfillment of the prophecy in Isa. 28:11-12, which describes it as a "rest" or "refreshing" even though others might not "hear." Paul's admonitions here seem to clearly imply he was concerned about their abuse of the gift in stated meetings ["when ye come together" (I Cor. 14:26)]. He was bothered by the women's speaking (v. 33-35), the lack of decorum in a service (v. 26-33), neglect of other gifts (v. 22-25), contentment without edification or education (v. 3-22), and possibly

[2] W.S. Boardman, *In the Power of the Spirit.*

other abuses. But in all his "negatives" there are clearly some positives. One of them is that tongues are for personal edification and that the church should never forbid their use.

2. For edifying the church. I Cor. 14 in its entirety leaves no room for mistake. The use of tongues is also for edifying the church, when there is interpretation. Paul wants those who have the gift to "excel" by using the gift to edify the church. The personal gift can, therefore, by development, be nurtured in such a way that that same gift can be used to edify the church. It is clear from I Cor. 14:5 that if an interpreter is present, tongues can be just as edifying as prophecy.

Irving, in the early days of Pentecostalism, emphasized prophecy over tongues, making it the "supreme gift," just as Pentecostals today emphasize tongues as the supreme gift, even to making it the "initial evidence" of the baptism of the Holy Spirit. If practiced in the will and purpose of God, who is to say what gift is better than another? But it is certain that this second use, to edify the church, is a higher, better use of the gift. Paul says, "Seek that ye may excel to the edifying of the church."

3. A sign to the unbeliever. The first two uses of this gift are plainly for the Christian. But just as plainly, God designed a use with the unsaved in mind. The Christian has the gift, but the use is for the unsaved. A "sign" is something "significant." Of what? In every use of the miraculous signs and wonders in scripture, it was a credential, a validation, an attestation. Thus even unbelievers may recognize the presence of God in these gifts. There is no guarantee of this, as verse 21 clearly indicates, but it is another way God in His mercy and love speaks to the unsaved. To our knowledge, this is the only way tongues are used as a "sign," and that is *for the unsaved.*

For a group of Christians to stand around a seeker watching his lips to see if he speaks in tongues, is an abuse of this gift, "wherefore tongues are for a sign, not to them that believe . . . " A Christian who looks for another to speak in tongues as a "sign of the baptism" is biblically out of order. This use of the "sign-gift" needs no interpretation; it would not be understood by the unsaved anyway. But, if someone he *knows* cannot speak his language, his native tongue, rises to bring a message in tongues where he is there in the service, this is significant.

I could take you on such a tour of all nine of the gifts and show you from the New Testament as well as from experience today, that each gift has its use—and its abuse. Each gift has its potential blessing and purpose for the believer and the unbeliever. Used aright, these gifts are for the church today and for the world.

Years ago I accepted the pastorate of a little Baptist church in the state of Maine. This Baptist church and a little Pentecostal church were the only ones in town. The young Pentecostal pastor came to his first church about the same time I came to the Baptist church. I visited him in his home, and we established a friendship. We had joint prayer meetings and street meetings. We swapped pulpits and worked together in many ways. Both churches began to grow in spirit and numbers.

One night my wife and I visited his church unannounced. A very small number of people were assembled. During the song service, the young pastor raised his eyes to heaven and let out a volley of words in some strange language. Although unfamiliar with the practice, I did recognize it as a message in tongues. It was quite lengthy, and soon after came the interpretation. Even as an independent, fundamentalist, separationist Baptist, I had never before felt the witness of the Spirit so strong in my soul. Oh, what strength and encouragement and blessing it was as he prophesied, "God will be with you in your ministry here. Trust in Him. Be not afraid, though there will be those who oppose you . . . "

I sat there, melted in His presence. I just *knew* God was speaking to me. *No dispensationalist can take that away from me, nor can he call it a curse, nor can he say it was Satan, nor can he say I am a Jew.*

While pastoring this same church, I counseled a young wife of only a few months who was having marital difficulties. She came into my study one day in tears. It seems she and her husband could not decide which church to go to regularly.

"I like it here," she began; "the people are wonderful. I was saved in this church. But in my husband's church (Pentecostal) the messages in tongues so often seem just for me, even though I do not speak in tongues myself. They are so helpful, and the people here just don't have these gifts. I guess we just don't believe in them." As her pastor I could do nothing other than advise her to go with her husband. She wanted to go where the demonstration of power was—and I couldn't blame her.

It was at this same pastorate, that I once conducted a funeral in a little country cemetery near West Ripley, Me. One tombstone epitaph read:

> "I came without my own consent,
> Lived a few years, much discontent,
>   At human errors grieving.
> I ruled myself by reasons laws
> But I got contempt and not applause
>   Because of disbelieving.
> For nothing could e'er me convert
> To faith some people did assert
>   Alone would bring salvation.
> But now the grave does me enclose,
> The superstitious will suppose
>   I'm doomed to hell's damnation.
> But as to that they do not know;
> Opinions oft from ignorance flow
>   Devoid of sure foundation.
> 'Tis easy men should be deceived
> When anything's by them believed
>   Without a demonstration."

Some might comment, "Oh, the humanist depravity!" But, I see more! In fact, I hear an honest heart crying for "reality"! If he had only seen a "demonstration" of faith that "some people" only "asserted", he might well have joined Thomas and cried "My Lord and My God!"

CHAPTER VI

THE GIFTS FOR TODAY

One author says, "The Pentecostal gifts of the Spirit recorded in Acts 2:1-4 and Acts 3 are not necessarily for today. Hebrews 2:4 indicates that the gifts involved were evidential for the opening days of the Christian church so that the people who had no written New Testament might have grounds for faith in Christ." After that validation occurred, the sign-gifts were supposedly no longer necessary, and since God never works wonders simply to entertain people, they just vanished.

Quite a philosophy.

Does this author think that just because the canon of scriptures was completed that everyone *had* the scriptures to read and ponder? It was not until around 1500 years *after* Christ that printing was invented. Therefore there were no books, not even the Bible, that anyone could read and study. People did not even know how to read, for there was little purpose in learning to read since there were no books. Only a few scribes had a precious few manuscripts, papyruses or scrolls; nothing existed for the common people. Alas, they still did not have the Word of God, even though the canon was complete at about 100 A.D.

Gutenberg did not come along to change that situation until some 1400 years later. And it was many years after Gutenberg before any significant percentage of the people learned to read. We can safely say that it has been only in the last 300 years that the people have actually "had" the Bible. Can it thus be reasoned that the *written* word was completed, and they no longer needed miracles, signs, and wonders?

Further, we might be surprised to find out how many homes even now do not have a Bible in them. Recently in our city some parents were enraged because their children came home from school bringing Gideon New Testaments. They even wrote letters to the newspaper stating they were incensed at having the Bibles in their homes. Are they any different from people in Jesus' day or the apostolic period? They both are (were) without the Word; both are (were) in need of proof that God is not dead.

The gifts did vanish—they disappeared. But was it because the Bible canon was completed? Or did Christians lose the gifts due to lack of faith, and an emphasis on worldliness and ritual? Was it God's fault or theirs? And then what accounts for the contemporary return of the gifts among people of all denominations as they surrender their wills (and tongues) to the Lord Jesus?

The dispensationalist bases his whole system on this one idea: that the gifts vanished from the experience of the church, therefore they were no longer needed. Yet he never seems to consider why they vanished. Strange, indeed, since all dispensationalists agree that no one should twist his Bible to fit some experience he has had; rather, his experience must be in accord with the Bible teaching. If it's wrong to base one's view of the scripture on their experience, it's wrong to base it on *lack of experience! It isn't right to assume that the reason we don't have these gifts is because we aren't sup-posed to have them.* I could show where the present-day church doesn't have New Testament love (agape) as Jesus taught it. Does this mean we are not supposed to have love? I know a great many dispensationalists who are possessed by fear and insecurity. Does this mean that Jesus intends for them to live this way? And what about the fact that there is little peace in the world today? Is this because we are not supposed to strive after peace?

Church history clearly records the facts about the waning power of the church. Thomas Payne, in his book, *The Covenant Promise of the Father,* described the whole sad story:

" . . . for as a result of this special baptism of divine power it has by God been decreed, that His Son shall have the heathen for his inheritance, and the uttermost parts of the earth for His possession. . . . Had the early church not degen-erated and become worldly, had it not ignored and made sacrifice of this special promise of the Holy Ghost, what mighty inroads would have been made into the Kingdom of Satan. But instead of this special influence of the Holy Spirit being exceedingly prized, and with prayer and self-sacrifice diligently sought and obtained, it soon became with the early church a thing of little or no account. That is, the fiery days of persecution once ended, the former entire dependence upon the upholding power of the Holy Spirit speedily declined, while under our ever increasing degree of worldly mindedness, cumbrous forms and pompous ritual became the things really sought after and esteemed. Thus the Holy Spirit was continually grieved and dishonoured and His powerful influence (as the express promise of the Father) most sinfully sacrificed." [1]

This is the real reason why the Holy Spirit's manifestations vanished. This was "revival in reverse." The very things we need for revival today are the very things the early church gradually lost and relinquished. The supernatural, with the gifts, signs, and wonders, left the church's ministry, indeed, but still man tries to excuse himself from the obvious responsibility, knowing it is all too clear there is now no evidence of power in the church.

But I must speak; I cannot hold my peace with my growing conviction that the answer to today's religious rigidity, formal worship, empty churches, and sterile irrelevancy—is miracle.

John Wesley put it this way:

"It does not appear that these extraordinary gifts of the Holy Ghost were common in the church for more than two or three centuries. We seldom hear of them after that fatal period when the emperor Constantine called himself a Christian . . . from this time they almost totally ceased. . . . The Christians had no more of the Spirit of Christ than the heathens. . . . This was the real cause why the extraordinary gifts of the Holy Ghost were no longer to be found in the Christian church; because the Christians were turned heathen again, and had only a dead form left." [2]

William B. Riley, one of the "fighting fundamentalists,"

---

[1] Thomas Payne, *The Covenant Promise of the Father.*

[2] John Wesley, *Works* (Grand Rapids, Mich.: Zondervan, 1958), 7:26-27.

opposed modernism in his own Baptist schools with a fervor unequaled even in modern times. Concerning the gifts, he wrote:

"That such a tongue existed in the New Testament experience cannot be sanely disproved; that the gifts of the New Testament times were intended for all ages is not the subject of doubt with some of us. With Gordon we affirm that it is impossible for us to look at that rich cluster of promises that hang by a single stem in Mark 16:16-18, and pluck out what suits us, declaring that the rest of them obtained only for a short time. Such treatment of the Word of God is unworthy the sincere students of the Bible. The 'gift' is there, and the 'gift' may be here." [3]

Riley mentioned Gordon. A.J. (Adoniram Judson) Gordon founded the Gordon College of Theology and Missions in Boston, now known as the Gordon-Conwell Theological Seminary. A.J. Gordon says:

"We have maintained in the previous chapter that the Baptism in the Holy Ghost was given once for all on the day of Pentecost, when the Paraclete came in person to make His abode in the church. It does not follow therefore that every believer has received this baptism. God's gift is one thing; our appropriation of that gift is quite another thing. . . . It seems clear from the scriptures that it is still the duty and privilege of believers to receive the Holy Spirit by a conscious, definite act of appropriating faith, just as they received Jesus Christ. . . . There is the same reason for accepting him for his special ministry as for accepting the Lord Jesus for his special ministry. . . . We must withhold our consent from the inconsistent exegesis which would make the water baptism of the apostolic times still rigidly binding, but would relegate the baptism in the Spirit to a bygone dispensation." [4]

(An interesting note: one group of ultradispensationalists have actually done just what Gordon intimates, that is, they have relegated water baptism to a bygone transition period and scrapped the practice rather than accept the truth

<hr/>

[3] William B. Riley, *Bible of the Expositor and the Evangelist* (Cleveland, Ohio: Union Gospel Press, 1926).

[4] A.J. Gordon, *The Ministry of the Spirit* (Philadelphia, Pa.: American Baptist Publication Society, 1894), p. 67-68, 72.

that if they accept the command of Jesus to baptize in water they also have to accept his command to be baptized in the Holy Spirit.)

Gordon's emphasis is that one must accept the Spirit for His work, just as they accept Christ for His work for them. Universalism teaches that all men are saved just because Christ died for all men, relieving them of any responsibility to do anything about receiving Christ personally. The dispensationalists, using the same argument, say the same thing about the Christian's relationship with the Holy Spirit, saying that just because the Holy Spirit was given means that automatically all Christians have Him. True, "if any man hath not the Spirit of Christ, he is none of His" (Rom. 8:9). Every Christian is indwelt by the Spirit, but as for receiving the baptism of the Holy Spirit, dispensationalists use the universalist argument to bolster their thesis!

Andrew Murray, a great man of God out of the past, says:

"This Baptism of the Spirit is the crown and glory of Jesus' work, that we need it, and must know that we have it, if we are to live the true Christian life. We need it. The Holy Jesus needed it. Christ's loving, obedient disciples needed it. It is something more than the working of the Spirit in regeneration. It is the personal Spirit of Christ making Him present within us, always abiding in the heart in the power of His glorified nature, as He is exalted above every enemy. It is the Spirit of the life of Christ Jesus making us free from the law of sin and death, and bringing us, as a personal experience, into the liberty from sin to which Christ redeemed us, but which to so many regenerate is only a blessing registered on their behalf, but not possessed or enjoyed. It is the enduement with power to fill us with boldness in the presence of every danger, and give the victory over the world and every enemy. . . . To the disciples the Baptism of the Spirit was very distinctly not His first bestowal for regeneration, but the definite communication of the presence in power of their glorified Lord. . . . Just as there was a twofold operation of the one Spirit in the Old and New Testaments, of which the state of the disciples before and after Pentecost was the most striking illustration, so there may be, and in the majority of Christians, is, a corresponding difference of experience. . . . When once the distinct recognition of what the indwelling of the Spirit was meant to bring is brought home to the soul, and [he] is ready to give up all to be made partaker of it, the believer may ask and expect what may be termed a Baptism of the Holy Spirit." [5]

The church today is starving for teaching like that. But we are being robbed just as surely as if they had their hands in the till of our coffers.

Some years ago, in the tabernacle at the Word of Life Camp on Schroon Lake, New York, Charles E. Fuller was the featured speaker. In spite of his dispensational surroundings he electrified the audience with his simple forthright statement declaring that one Sunday shortly before that time, right after going off the air at his Los Angeles radio rally of the Old-Fashioned Revival Hour, someone arose and began speaking in tongues. He motioned for quiet from the rest of the congregation. After the message Charles Fuller said, "Soon, someone arose and gave a beautiful interpretation, a beautiful interpretation." Fuller went on to plead with the people at Word of Life Camp not to be afraid of the Holy Spirit's working.

The Full Gospel Business Men's Fellowship International has published a booklet, compiled by Jerry Jensen, entitled, *Baptists and the Baptism of the Holy Spirit.* The author tells the story of several Baptist preachers, laymen, and laywomen who have come into the charismatic movement and under the power of the Holy Spirit have moved out into extensive ministries. Similar booklets are also available on Methodists, Presbyterians, Episcopalians, etc.

I know of many others, Baptists particularly, who as pastors are bringing their churches into the full light of this renewal. One of them is my good friend, Jamie Buckingham, who is better known to reading America as an author and writer. A Southern Baptist pastor, he is now leading a rapidly growing flock of people from all denominations in a "body ministry" in Melbourne, Florida. His church has broken denominational ties and is growing more rapidly than any other "church" I know of in the state. Occasionally I visit in this open congregation which has no formal membership and

[5] Andrew Murray, *The Spirit of Christ* (New York: Revell, 1888), p. 29, 323.

is composed of hundreds of people from all main-line denominations who have been Spirit-baptized. I see "hippie" looking young people by the hundreds with Bibles under their arms and the sparkle of Christ in their eyes. I see black and white lifting their arms in praise together. I hear the gifts of the spirit in operation—tongues, interpretation, prophecy; and I see healings and miracles take place. It's not unusual at the close of the service (or sometimes at the beginning of the service if the Holy Spirit directs) for the pastor (or whoever else may be leading at that moment) to "give an invitation." Only instead of asking people to close their eyes and bow their heads, the congregation sits alert and expectant as first one and then another rises to his feet and says, "Today I accept Christ as my Savior and make public my belief in Him as my Lord." Statements like this are nearly always followed with great rejoicing on the part of the congregation, praising God, and often spontaneous applause. At other times people will come to the altar or members of the Body will circulate in the congregation, laying on hands and praying for others to be healed or receive the baptism of the Holy Spirit. Yet all things are done decently and in order, and even though these may seem foreign to my background, I thrill to my soul as I feel the Holy Spirit ministering as He did in those early church services in catacombs and upper rooms. The ministry here is vindicated (for those who demand proof in results) by increased ministries (many from this congregation have resigned their jobs and gone to foreign and home mission fields), souls won to Christ, families reunited, and gloom replaced with joy in the believers. Driving back across the state to my home I constantly find myself asking the question, "Why aren't more pastors and Christian workers receiving and using these beautiful gifts of the Spirit?"

Yet I know the reason why. Teaching. Roy L. Laurin says, "Unless at this point we distinguish between the experience of the apostles and the teachings of the apostles, we will be greatly confused. . . . In other words, let us not teach the experience of the apostles in relation to the Holy Spirit, but let us experience the teaching of the apostles."[6]

[6] Roy L. Laurin, *Be Filled with the Spirit* (Los Angeles: American Prophetic League), p. 21.

So, don't teach their experiences, but experience their teachings. Shall we bring the fallacy of this into sharp focus and remind you this means exactly, "Don't do as I do, but do as I say?" The obvious hypocrisy of this is all too obvious to me.

If the apostles' experience is not for us today, why are these experiences recorded for us in the Bible? Just to get us confused? Have you ever stopped to think?—it would have been the simplest thing in the world for God to have left out those portions where miracles were performed. The Holy Spirit could have easily kept Paul from writing I Cor. 14 and Luke from writing those portions of Acts. Without those words there would be no controversy today. If He had wanted us all to be dispensationalists, why did He put Acts 2:39 in the Bible?

I maintain that if healing, tongues, and deliverance are not for us today, then God made a colossal blunder when He allowed those things in the canon of scripture. If He had not told us all about it, I would never have known about it. Perhaps we should just forbid our children to read this section of the Bible since it has no meaning for us today.

A.E. Bishop, way back in 1920, wrote *Tongues, Signs and Visions Not God's Order for Today* with a very commendatory foreword by C.I. Scofield. In Bishop's own introduction he says, "Some of the most renowned Bible teachers of the world have been very kind in answering my questions relating to the miracles and sign-gifts and all are unanimous in believing that the sign-gifts were divinely removed after having accomplished their purposes in the beginning of the present dispensation."[7] With the advent of present charismatic renewal in churches of all denominations, he would have to "pick and choose" his men now.

This underscores our point: The scholars are just the reason why we do not have the gifts as we ought today. Not particularly the men, of course, but what they taught. This devastating doctrine that God divinely removed the gifts has surely continued to rob us.

---

[7] A.E. Bishop, *Tongues, Signs and Visions Not God's Order for Today* (Los Angeles: Biola Book Room, 1920), p. 5.

CHAPTER VII

THE BAPTISM OF THE HOLY SPIRIT

"It was the closing day of the Northfield students' conference, the gathering of the students from the eastern colleges. Mr. Moody (D.L. Moody) asked me to preach on Saturday night and on Sunday morning on the Baptism of the Holy Ghost. On Saturday night I had spoken about 'The Baptism with the Holy Ghost, What it is, What it does, The need of it and the Possibility of it.' On Sunday morning I spoke on 'The Baptism with the Holy Spirit: How to get it.' It was just exactly twelve o'clock when I finished my morning sermon, and I took out my watch and said, 'Mr. Moody has invited us all to go up on the mountain at three o'clock this afternoon to pray for the power of the Holy Spirit. It is three hours to three o'clock. Some of you cannot wait three hours. You do not need to wait. Go to your rooms; go out into the woods; go to your tent; to anywhere you can get alone with God and have this matter out with Him.'

"At three o'clock we all gathered in front of Mr. Moody's mother's house (she was then still living) and then we began to pass down the lane, through the gate up on the mountainside. There were four hundred and fifty six of us in all; I know the number because Paul Moody counted us as we passed through the gate. After a while Mr. Moody said, 'I don't think we need to go any further, let us sit down here.' We sat down on stumps and logs on the ground. Mr. Moody said, 'Have any of you students anything to say?' I think about 75 of them arose, one after another, and said, 'Mr. Moody, I could not wait until three o'clock; I have been alone with God since the morning service, and I believe I have a right to say that I have been baptized with the Holy Spirit.' When these testimonies were over, Mr. Moody said, 'Young men, I cannot see any reason why we should not kneel down right here now and ask God that the Holy Spirit may fall upon us just as definitely as He fell upon the apostles on the day of Pentecost. Let us pray.' And we did pray there on the mountainside. As we had gone up the mountainside heavy clouds had been gathering, and just as we began to pray those clouds broke and the raindrops began to fall through the overhanging pines. But there was another cloud that had been gathering over Northfield for ten days, a cloud big with the mercy and grace and power of God; and as we began to pray, our prayers seemed to pierce the cloud and the Holy Ghost fell upon us. Men and women, that is what we all need—the Baptism with the Holy Ghost." [1]

If I or any other fundamentalist pastor should do anything like this today we would be branded as the worst of fanatics. We would be labeled "holy rollers." Every theological eye within distance would be casting suspicion on our entire ministry. *Yet may God grant the day when once again godly pastors will lead their flocks into this biblical experience, this continuation of the Book of Acts, this personal and church-wide revival so sorely needed.* I would be willing to encounter some wildfire, and deal with it, if only we had the real fire once more.

I find another lesson in the above recounting of this Northfield experience, that is, that every experience must be based on the Word of God. It was after Torrey's two Bible sermons that true results followed. I have visited all too many Pentecostal churches, and most recently too many "charismatic" denominational churches, without hearing any sermons like the one Torrey preached at Northfield. No wonder the fire fell out there in the field; the fuel had already been poured out in the sermon.

How many pastors, next Sunday morning, would have a very much unexpected, unannounced deacons' meeting if they preached on "The Baptism of the Holy Spirit: How to Get It"? But the revival that everybody is talking about and so pitifully few are receiving will come only when men like R.A. Torrey arrive on the scene and start teaching from the

[1] R.A. Torrey, *Why God Used D.L. Moody* (Chicago: Moody Press, 1923), p. 63. Now published by "Sword of the Lord."

Bible exactly what Torrey, Moody, Finney, Gordon, Mueller, Simpson, Murray, and others taught and experienced. Torrey put his finger on it when he said, "Men and women, that is what we all need—the Baptism with the Holy Ghost."

the Edict of Nantes, which had given religious liberty, he strove by dragonades to drive Protestants into the Roman Catholic church. The Huguenots were led by John Cavalier, a farmer, into inaccessible mountains. *Among these persecuted people were those who spoke in tongues. There are records, both by enemies and by friends as to their prophetic gifts.* Prophets came from the Cavennes to Holland, and on to Germany. At that time among professors and students there was a great receptivity to God's power. *In 1714 they brought the gifts of tongues and prophecy to Wetterau, near Frankfurt-on-Main.* Their leaders were an ejected Wurtemburg pastor named Gruber and a brother Rock, a saddler. They and their 'gifted' followers were called the inspired ones of the Wetterau."[12] (Italics supplied.)

John Wesley and His Followers, 1703-1791 A.D.

The name of the Rev. John Wesley, preacher, evangelist, teacher, scholar, and author, is synonymous with Methodism. He is well known in Protestant church history as the leader of the Great Revival and Evangelical movement in England in the eighteenth century, out of which emerged the Methodist denomination. He was keenly aware of the reality of the miraculous gifts of the Spirit. He certainly did not deny the gifts or the validity of tongues. On the contrary, he explained why there had been an absence or lack of these marvelous manifestations at certain times in the history of Christianity. It was because the so-called organized Christians had only a dead form of worship, denying the power of the Holy Spirit, their love having waxed as cold as the heathen. Wesley in his sermon, "The More Excellent Way," described the situation this way:

"It does not appear that these extraordinary gifts of the Holy Ghost were common in the Church for more than two or three centuries. We seldom hear of them after that fatal period when the Emperor Constantine called himself a Christian, and from a vain imagination of promoting the Christian cause, thereby heaped riches and power and honour upon the Christians in general, but in particular upon Chris-

[12]*Ibid.*, 1:2 (November 1966): 15.

tian clergy. From this time they almost totally ceased; very few instances of the kind being found. *The cause of this was not, as has been vulgarly supposed, because there is no more occasion for them, because all the world were become Christians.* This is a miserable mistake, not a twentieth part of it was then nominally Christian. *The real cause was: the love of many, almost all Christians, so-called, was waxed cold. The Christians had no more the Spirit of Christ than the other heathens; the Son of Man when He came to examine His Church could hardly find faith. This was the real cause why the extraordinary gifts of the Holy Ghost were no longer to be found in the Christian Church; because the Christians were turned heathen again and had only a dead form left."*[13] (Italics supplied.)

So it is today. God will not pour out of His Spirit and the supernatural gifts on those parts or persons of His professing Church who have waxed cold, turned heathen, and have only a dead form left! But praise His Holy Name, Jesus Christ is baptizing in the Holy Spirit all believers who have not lost their first love, who are turning away from dead forms and ritual, and who are hungering and thirsting in love and faith and obedience to receive the fullness of God's supernatural power. Then they will truly be enabled to deny themselves, take up their crosses, and follow Him to accomplish the Father's end-time work, which is now in progress.

Wesley's Refutation of Dr. Middleton

John Wesley also refuted an attack on the supernatural gifts of the Spirit made by a certain Dr. Middleton, who wrote that there was no record or history after apostolic times of one instance where any particular person had ever exercised or pretended to exercise the gift of tongues in any age or country. (How wrong and misled by traditional teaching and doctrine was Dr. Middleton is shown by the authorities quoted or referred to herein!) Wesley wrote this vigorous refutation and protest: "Sir, your memory fails you again—it (speaking with tongues) has been heard MORE THAN ONCE no further off than the valleys of Dauphiny."[14]

[13]*Loc. cit.*
[14]*Ibid.,* p. 15-16.

Other Wesley Converts

During the great Wesleyan Revival there was an outpouring by God of His Spirit with the accompanying gifts. The *Encyclopaedia Britannica* states: "If, however, the inarticulate utterances of ecstatic joy are followed, as they were in some of Wesley's converts, by a life of devoted holiness, we should hesitate to say that they may not bear some analogy to those of the Corinthian Christians."[15]

Thomas Walsh, 1750 A.D.

In the diary of Thomas Walsh, one of Wesley's foremost preachers, dated March 8, 1750, are these words: "This morning the Lord gave me a language that I knew not of, raising my soul to Him in a wonderful manner."[16] *This is more of that,* occurring 1700 years after Pentecost!

Nineteenth Century

MacDonald Brothers, 1830 A.D.

According to the life story of the MacDonald Brothers by a Dr. Robert Norton, M.D., published in 1840, the Holy Spirit fell upon these brothers in the year 1830 in accordance with Acts 2:4 in this manner: "A few evenings after the above occurrence, *during a prayer meeting, George, in whom nothing supernatural had ever previously appeared, and whose natural condition had made him the least of the family to welcome the supernatural manifestations in others, began suddenly to speak in an unknown tongue.* James followed him, and thus commenced that speaking in tongues and prophesying which never afterwards wholly ceased."[17] (Italics supplied.) *This* is more of *that* occurring 1800 years after Pentecost!

Edmund (or Edward) Irving, 1792-1834, A.D.

Leader of the Irvingites, Irving was a Scotch-Presbyterian preacher in London. He received the baptism in the Holy

[15] *Ibid.,* p. 16.
[16] *Loc. cit.*
[17] *Loc. cit.*

Spirit, spoke in other tongues, and preached and manifested in his ministry the other early apostolic gifts of the Spirit, including prophesying and healing by faith. For these beliefs he was ousted from the Presbyterian Church. His revivals, however, without the aid of the organized church but by the fire, power, and love of the Holy Spirit, bore abundant fruit for the eternal Kingdom of God. It is reported that this saintly man of God led thousands to Christ. His revival audiences ranged from 6,000 to 12,000. *This* is more of the fruit of *that*.

Sweden, U.S.A., and Ireland, 1840-1850 A.D.

"The revival movement known as the 'Readers' of Sweden in 1841-43, had the gift of tongues in their worship. The 'Gift Adventists' (not [to be confused with] Seventh Day Adventists) had this gift among them in our own New England States before the Civil War. Many spoke in tongues in the Irish revivals of 1850."[18]

Charles G. Finney, 1792-1875 A.D.

Finney began his career as a lawyer. After his conversion, he became an evangelist. He "is regarded as one of the greatest Revivalists of history. In this year [1844] his efforts yielded 50,000 converts per week for ten weeks, a total of 5,000,000 [sic, i.e., 500,000] conversions to Christ. He is the only evangelist credited with retaining 75 percent of his converts to the end. When the Finney Revival commenced in U.S.A. there were 200,000 church members, when it was completed there were 3,000,000 church members."[19]

Finney's Testimony as to Pentecostal Gifts

In his autobiography, Finney relates an experience exactly like that of speaking in unknown tongues: "I received a mighty baptism of the Holy Ghost. Without any expectation of it, without ever having the thought in my mind that there was such a thing for me, without any recollection that I have heard the thing mentioned by any person in the world, the

[18] *Loc. cit.*
[19] *Loc. cit.*

Holy Spirit descended upon me in a manner that seemed to go through me, body and soul. I could feel the impression like a wave of electricity going through and through me. Indeed, it seemed to come in waves of liquid love; for I could not express it in any other way. It seemed like the very breath of God. I can recollect distinctly that it seemed to fan me like immense wings. No words can express the wonderful love that was shed abroad in my heart. I wept aloud with joy and love; *and I do not know, but I should say I literally bellowed out the inutterable gushings of my heart.* These waves came over me, and over me, one after the other, until I recollect I cried out, 'I shall die if these waves continue to pass over me.' I said, 'Lord, I cannot bear any more.' Yet I had no fear of death . . . Thus I continued, till late at night I received some sound repose. When I awoke in the morning the sun had risen, and was pouring a clear light into my room. Words cannot express the impression that this sunlight made on me. Instantly the baptism I had received the night before returned upon me in the same manner. I arose upon my knees in the bed and wept aloud with joy, and remained for some time too much overwhelmed with the baptism of the Spirit to do anything but pour out of my soul to God."[20] Again we see recurring within the last 150 years *this* same mighty baptism by immersion in the Holy Spirit of which Joel and Peter spoke. And what tremendous fruit resulted!

I was astonished at some of the similarities in my own baptism in the Spirit with those of Finney, when I first read a portion of his memoirs many months later. In parts of his testimony it was as if I was reading and hearing afresh my own experience. It confirmed the reality of my experience, although there was never any doubt in my mind that it was all of God.

Peter MacKenzie, 1878 A.D.

"The celebrated Peter MacKenzie, writing to a Mr. Elliott from Leeds on February 5, 1878, said: 'I was in old Circuit last Sabbath, of Padiham. The place was packed, one of the largest and best loved feasts I have ever held. *The Holy Ghost*

[20]*Ibid.,* p. 16-17.

came down and the gift of tongues was surely granted. Oh, the power, melting, moving, saving, sanctifying.' "[21] (Italics supplied.)

Dwight L. Moody, 1837-1899, A.D.

Dwight L. Moody in the latter half of the nineteenth century was as preeminent and effective as an evangelist and soul winner for God as was Finney in the middle half of the century. His teamwork with Ira David Sankey, the singer, in making Gospel hymns popular as a means of stirring audiences is well known. Moody Bible Institute in Chicago is a continuing tribute to the several foundations which Moody laid for Christian education.

Moody had the baptism in the Holy Spirit. Morris Plotts in *Herald of Faith* had this to say: "The well-known evangelist, Dwight L. Moody, enjoyed the gift of tongues according to John Davidson, the designer of the Scofield Bible, who was intimately acquainted with him." [22]

Moody's formal education ended when he was thirteen. Without the enabling and empowering gifts of the Holy Spirit, including tongues, it is obvious that his prodigious accomplishments for the Lord could not have occurred (Acts 1:8). As an example, we read the following observation of a "Rev. R. Boyd, D.D. (Baptist), who was a very intimate friend of Moody: 'When I (a Y.M.C.A. member) got to the rooms of the Young Men's Christian Association (Victoria Hall, London), *I found the meeting 'on fire'. The young men were speaking with tongues, prophesying. What on earth did it mean? Only that Moody had been addressing them that afternoon!* What manner of man is this? thought I, but still I did not give him my hand ... Many of the clergy were so opposed to the movement that they turned their backs upon our poor innocent Young Men's Christian Association for the part we took in the work; but afterward when the flood-gates of divine grace were opened, Sunderland (near London) was taken by storm. I cannot describe Moody's great meeting: I can only say that the people of Sunderland warmly sup-

[21]*Ibid.*, p. 17.
[22] *Loc. cit.*

ported the movement, in spite of their local spiritual advisers.' "[23] (Italics supplied.)

In the *Moody Monthly* for March, 1933, there is an article about Dwight L. Moody that reads:

"Pentecost and that for which it stands is a vast and undiscovered continent to much of Christendom today. It needs rediscovering. A recent church report stated that 7,500 churches in the United States reported not one member added to the church on confession of faith. That means 780,000 sermons not producing a single conversion, while Peter's one sermon on the day of Pentecost resulted in the conversion of some 3,000 souls.

"There is no need of the Church's being void of power when there stands before the throne of God 'the sevenfold Spirit of God' with all the divine fullness of power. 'Pentecost' may mean to many of us 'plenty-of-cost,' but it is worth any price to get the power."[24]

Not long ago a young man who had just graduated from Moody Bible Institute and its pilot training course came to my law office in Los Angeles for consultation. After the legal matter was disposed of we enjoyed a wonderful fellowship in the Lord. During the course of our sharing I asked him if they at Moody Bible Institute had ever taught or told him that Dwight L. Moody had received the baptism in the Holy Spirit and the gift of speaking in other tongues, as well as other gifts of the Spirit. He replied, "no," that he had never so much as heard of such things! Then I shared with him my own experiences and the supporting Scriptures and how my life in Jesus Christ had been enriched and made more fruitful thereby. I also gave him some literature on the baptism. Then I prayed that the seeds of truth which the Holy Spirit had planted would take root, opening his eyes and heart to the reality of the baptism and the gifts for today.

About six months later I met him unexpectedly at a Christian fellowship gathering in a private home. He had a new radiance and joy about him that had not been evident at our first meeting. Upon inquiry I learned from a mutual Spirit-filled brother in Christ who had brought him to the

[23] *Loc. cit.*
[24] *Moody Monthly,* March 1933, p. 340.

meeting what had happened. This young man had become so hungry to know more about the baptism and the power of Pentecost that he sought others for guidance and confirmation. Then he had sought Jesus the Baptizer, and Jesus in accordance with His Word had poured out the promise of the Father, the Holy Spirit, upon him with the gift of tongues. Praise the Lord for His goodness!

William Booth, 1829-1912 A.D.

This great man of God was converted at age fifteen, became a preacher and subsequently the founder of the Salvation Army in 1878. The abounding and continuing fruit of this worldwide Christian organization, especially in saving and serving the unfortunate and underprivileged, is well known and recognized the world over.

That this outstanding servant of God recognized that no man could do great exploits for the Lord without the operation of the supernatural gifts of the Spirit is demonstrated in this account by Booth, reprinted two years after his death in *War Cry,* the Salvation Army publication, for November 11, 1914:

"A good deal of attention is given to what we know as the extraordinary 'gifts of the Spirit,' that is, the ability to do something which is beyond the power of man to do without the direct operation of God.

"Such gifts as these were, without doubt, possessed by the Apostles ... *They had the gift of tongues, that is, they received suddenly the power to speak languages they had never learned. They had the 'Gift of healing,' they cured the sick, opened the eyes of the blind, unstopped the ears of the deaf and restored the dead to life instantaneously without the use of ordinary means.* They wrought miracles, they caused events to happen that were contrary to the laws of nature.

"These were remarkable gifts proving that God was with them, *because no man could do these things unless God was operating directly through him.*

"These gifts were useful, inasmuch as they called attention to those who possessed them, declaring that the mission of these persons (Officers) was divine, and justified men everywhere in believing what they had to say.

"For this reason they were important to the world, and their possession today would be a great blessing to mankind. There is not a word in the Bible which proves we may not have them at the present time, and there is nothing in experience to show they would not be useful today as in any previous period of the Church's history. No man, therefore, can be condemned for desiring them, and the recent remarkable signs and wonders amongst us, not only demand but shall have our most profound and sympathetic considerations.

"It must never be forgotten that all real healing, whether of body or soul, whether accomplished in a moment or in a year of time, whether done apparently without or through the use of means, is like effected by the direct operation of God. It is God who saves and heals.

"It must be ever remembered that all gifts, ordinary or extraordinary alike, come from God . . .

"Far be it from me to say one word that would stay the longing of any heart for the extraordinary gifts already mentioned. *I long for them myself, I believe in their necessity, and I believe they are already among us."* [Italics supplied.] "By all means let us have the perfection of the Divine method of working.

"The poor infidel world should be made to see all of God that is possible, that it may believe." [Italics supplied.]

"Let us covet, let us seek earnestly, nay, let us never rest until we possess in all its fulness that celestial passion." [25]

Twentieth Century

It would not be possible in the scope of this presentation to show in depth the great outpourings of the Holy Spirit and the charismatic awakening in the United States and the world commencing near the beginning of this century. Many excellent books, pamphlets, and articles have been written touching on this subject. A few are:

> Brumback, Carl. *Suddenly . . . from Heaven.* Springfield, Missouri: Gospel Publishing House.

[25] William Booth, "Spiritual Gifts," *Logos Magazine,* 1:2 (November 1966): 18-19.

Christenson, Lawrence. *Speaking in Tongues.* Minneapolis, Minnesota: Bethany Fellowship, Inc.

Ervin, Howard M. *These Are Not Drunken as Ye Suppose.* Plainfield, New Jersey: Logos, 1968.

Frodsham, Stanley. *With Signs Following.* Springfield, Missouri: Gospel Publishing House, 1941.

Gee, Donald. *Spiritual Gifts in the Work of the Ministry Today.* Los Angeles: The L.I.F.E. Bible College Alumni Assn., 1963.

Horton, Harold. *The Gifts of the Spirit.* London: Assemblies of God Publishing House, 1954.

Kelsey, Morton T. *Tongue Speaking.* Garden City, New York: Doubleday & Co., Inc., 1964.

Kendrick, Klaude. *The Promise Fulfilled: A History of the Modern Pentecostal Movement.* Springfield, Missouri: Gospel Publishing House, 1961.

Nicol, John Thomas. *Pentecostalism.* Plainfield, N.J.: Logos, International. (This excellent book is probably the most comprehensive and authoritative history available of the worldwide Pentecostal movement. It contains a selective but extensive bibliography of books, articles, pamphlets, and other writings on this subject. The reader is referred to this bibliography for in-depth study of the movement.)

Sherrill, John. *They Speak with Other Tongues.* New York: McGraw-Hill, Inc., 1964.

Stiles, J.E. *The Gift of the Holy Spirit.* Burbank, California, n.d.

One thing is certain. A reading of the history of the Pentecostal movement, both as a new denominational stream of Christianity and also as a reviving force within the historic denominational churches, should convince any fair-minded Christian that here is the dynamic power of God needed for the end-time worldwide witness for Christ and work of the Holy Spirit in preparation for the soon coming of our Lord Jesus Christ.

Students of the history of the Christian church in the United States are undoubtedly aware of the great outpourings beginning, among other places, on Azusa Street in Los Angeles in 1906. I doubt, however, whether the average Christian layman is aware of them. I say this because I was one of the latter group who knew practically nothing of these great historic events in the flow. and development of the church of Jesus Christ.

The turn of the twentieth century marked the beginning of the greatest outpouring of the Holy Spirit and the accompanying gifts of the Spirit the world has ever known. From the time of the Civil War many Protestant denominational churches had become institutionalized, rich in property, increased in goods, buildings, and membership, but poor and blind in spirituality and power. Many had become examples of the Laodicean church, lukewarm, complacent, coldly formalistic, with no forceful preaching or emotion permitted. These conditions regrettably still exist today in many areas of the organized churches.

Ministers called of God had been removed and replaced by men formally trained in schools and seminaries who entered the ministry as a profession or occupation as one might enter law or medicine, not as a direct calling of God. It is a sad commentary that we find this condition all too prevalent today.

The scriptural prescription of congregational group singing and "making melody in your hearts to the Lord" (Eph. 5:19) began to give way to the religious tranquilizer of substitutionary singing by organized choirs. Here also today we find too few churches where the people themselves as a congregation really sing out with the Spirit in joyous union unto the Lord.

Already the "higher critics" and "modernists" in their ivory theological towers as well as in the pulpits had begun to tear away at some of the very cornerstones of the Gospel. They were denying or questioning such eternal truths as the Virgin Birth of Jesus Christ, and the redemptive power of His shed blood, and the fact of His bodily resurrection from the tomb. Again, how much of this anti-Christ spirit do we see and hear and read about today!

It was in this atmosphere of spiritual paralysis in the early 1900's that a great hunger and desire came into the hearts of a number of fearless men of God in the United States and elsewhere (put there, of course, by the blessed Holy Spirit Himself). This desire was to earnestly seek and receive the enduement from on high, the baptism in the Holy Spirit with the spiritual gifts received at Pentecost and thereafter, for the power and fire to stir up, revive, and renew a spiritually stagnated Church and start the rivers of living water running again. There is unmistakable evidence that this same desire is sweeping today into the hearts of hundreds of thousands of Christian laymen and clergy alike, across the world in all denominations, who are not satisfied with a sterile form of Christianity having no life or power.

Topeka, Kansas, 1900

In this year, a former Methodist minister named Charles F. Parham opened a Bible college in Topeka, Kansas, with about 40 students and operated on faith in God to supply every need. During a short absence from the school, he gave his students a special assignment to individually search the Scriptures carefully to determine if there was any special Bible evidence of the baptism in the Holy Spirit. When he returned, he asked, "What is the Bible evidence of the baptism in the Holy Spirit?" The students were unanimous in their decision, to wit, speaking in other tongues as the Spirit gave utterance was the outward manifestation on each occasion in the Apostolic church of the inward dwelling of or baptism in the Holy Spirit!

Thereafter, each member of the student body earnestly began to pray and expectantly seek the experience of the baptism as described in the Book of Acts. In a few days the Holy Spirit fell upon one of the women students who began speaking in a Chinese language. Classes were suspended in January, 1901, for continued prayer and seeking. Before long a majority testified they had experienced the baptism in the Holy Spirit and spoken in other tongues. With this empowering of the Holy Spirit many forthwith became evangelists and missionaries. Parham, himself, after much persecution from the established denominational churches and newspapers, went into preaching, teaching, and evangelistic campaigns, including a spectacular healing ministry in the states of Kansas, Missouri, and Texas. As a part of the fruit of his work in Texas alone, by 1905 it was estimated that there were 25,000 Pentecostal believers and 60 preachers of the now-termed "Full Gospel." The movement spread to other states.

Parham established another school in Houston, Texas, in

1905 similar to the Bethel Bible College in Topeka, using only the Bible as a textbook. One of his students was a one-eyed negro preacher named William J. Seymour.

Azusa Street Revival, Los Angeles. 1906.

In 1906, Evangelist Seymour was invited to come to Los Angeles from Texas to preach at a small mission church. He was an unprepossessing, plain, humble man, without pride, but with a burning spiritual message as to the reality and necessity of the experience of the 120 at Pentecost, even though he himself had not received the gift. He was a living example of God choosing the weak and foolish things of the world to confound the wise and mighty (I Cor. 1:27). This particular church rejected his sermon on Acts 2 as being relevant only for Pentecost and the time of the first-century church.

[Parenthetically, it is noteworthy that many churches are still resisting and rejecting the outpouring of the Holy Spirit today. But God knew this would occur. By the Holy Spirit, Stephen in A.D. 33 saw this rejection happening then and foresaw that resistance and opposition to the Holy Spirit would be occurring on occasions throughout the centuries of the church age. He exclaimed to the high priest and the men of the Jewish council or Sanhedrin, "You people, how stiffnecked (stubborn) you are (and pagan or heathen) at heart and deaf to the truth! You do always resist (and fight and oppose) the Holy Spirit, as your forefathers did!" (Acts 7:51). For telling them this truth he was stoned to death!]

The Azusa Street Revival had its beginning in a series of meetings in a private home in which a number of the participants received the Holy Spirit with the gift of tongues and with accompanying rejoicing and prayer. After a few days the group moved into a former livery stable on Azusa Street in a commercial section of downtown Los Angeles, which was an abandoned former meeting place of a Methodist church. Seymour was joined by others, and there, under low rafters and upon bare floors and planks laid on kegs for seats in a setting as unpretentious as the very manger of our blessed Lord, was born the renowned Azusa Street Revival.

Supernatural signs and wonders followed, confirming the

word with miraculous healings, deliverance, and exercise of the gifts of the Holy Spirit, including tongues (Mark 16:15-20). As the news of this outpouring spread, Christians throughout the United States and the world, hungry for more of the power of God and the demonstration of the Spirit (I Cor. 2:4-5) were drawn to Azusa Street. The magnitude of the convergence on this Faith Gospel Mission on Azusa Street was a living demonstration of the power and leading of the Holy Spirit to fill hungry hearts. Many who received the baptism were ministers and pastors who returned to their home churches full of the power and glory and joy of the Lord. From their ministries many others later received the baptism and became on fire for the Lord. This ultimately resulted in the establishment of over twenty-five new Pentecostal-type churches, preaching, teaching, and following the Full Gospel message. These included the Assemblies of God, the largest, the Church of God in Christ, Pentecostal Holiness, and Four-Square. These new churches were made up in large part of former members of the historic Protestant churches, including Presbyterians, Baptists, Lutherans, Methodists, and others. After receiving the baptism in the Holy Spirit they were either no longer welcome in, or no longer satisfied with, the lukewarm, powerless, uninspired Christianity of their own particular congregations, and sought fellowship and communion with others who were alive to God and walking in the Spirit.

Similarly, during these outpourings in the United States, men from foreign countries came, received, and went back to their native lands, where they established Full Gospel type churches, notably in South America and Italy. At about the same time there were independent outpourings of the Holy Spirit in Wales, England, the Scandinavian countries, Switzerland, India, Australia, and other parts of the world.

Great Welsh Revival — 1904 [26]

In 1904 there was a spiritual awakening in the relatively tiny community of Wales, England, which still stands as a

[26] Most of the material and all of the quotations in this section are taken from "Oh the Wonder of it All," by Kay Pernia, *Christ for the Nations* magazine, June 1968. For a fuller presentation of the Welsh Revival and its implications for the present-day movement of the Holy Spirit, the reader is referred to the whole article which contains many other observations and quotations.

mighty example of what can and will happen when born-again Christians unite in faithful and believing prayer for an outpouring of the Holy Spirit—the latter rain of Joel 2:23. The eyes of the Christian world were fastened upon Wales as the latter rain fell in such abundance as to flood the country.

Mrs. Jessie Penn-Lewis, well known, loved, and respected Christian writer, and one of the eyewitnesses of the Welsh Revival, wrote, "The Pentecostal character of the awakening in Wales is unmistakably clear. *Undoubtedly with this revival, we entered upon a new era of the world's history with supernatural workings of God such as have not been known since the days of the Early Church . . ."* [27]

Dr. Cynddylan Jones, commenting on the revival said, in part, referring to the startling question put by Paul to the Ephesians in about A.D. 56:

" 'Have ye received the Holy Ghost since ye believed?' was brought to the forefront through the Awakening. It is a question still loudly ringing out to the Church with tremendous consequences to a world dependent upon its being faced in truth by the people of God . . . *It is the call to the Church at the close of the dispensation to arise and receive the Pentecostal clothing of the Spirit which is her birthright and her need for an effectual witness of Christ in the world. What God did in Wales is an object lesson of what He is prepared to do for His people in every land, if they will seek His face and obey the conditions for His workings. If true members of Christ in every nation—be they few or many— were to receive what God means by a Baptism in the Holy Ghost and fire, signs and wonders would follow."* [28] (Italics supplied.)

World revival, according to Dr. Jones, really means the awakening and quickening of the people of God by the fire and power of the Holy Spirit—as he says, "a bending of the Christian." With this awakening will come the addition to the church by the Lord from the whole world "daily such as should be saved" (Acts 2:47; 4:4; 6:7). The Gospel then having been preached to every creature in the world in our generation (Mark 16:15), and the Great Commission as well

[27]*Ibid.,* p. 3.
[28]*Loc. cit.*

as all other prophetic prelude events having been fulfilled in our generation, nothing will then remain before the Lord will call his bride, the Church, from this earth to meet Him in the air (I Thess. 4:14-18).

Evan Roberts

That the baptism in the Holy Spirit was required and needed for the carrying out of the beginning of the end-time revival in Wales is shown in the remarkable life of Evan Roberts, a former coal miner whom God used as the catalyst and leader of the revival. After thirteen years of fervent prayer for a "visitation from God," he had a dramatic manifestation in 1904 in his own room in Loughor, Wales.

"The Holy Spirit manifested Himself in an overwhelming manner which filled my soul with divine awe. . . . I was lying in bed one day and felt vibrations; my body began to tremble. I got out of the bed, and as I was kneeling down by the bedside, I was lifted up and my lips began to move in utterances which cannot be described. There was a tremendous surging of joy that came over me."[29]

It is significant how closely the Pentecostal experience of the baptism in the Holy Spirit of Evan Roberts in Wales in 1904 paralleled the same experience of Charles G. Finney some eighty years earlier in Adams County, New York. We know that all do not receive the baptism in exactly the same manner, or place or intensity, the Lord being sovereign in His unlimited variety of methods. Yet we may be certain that unreported thousands throughout the centuries have received and are still receiving the baptism today in a manner similar to that experienced by Roberts and Finney. My own personal experience is an example. Several other members of the Body of Christ in the past five years have told me about similar experiences of receiving the baptism while alone in their own homes. Whatever the method, wherever the place, whoever the person, it is the same one Body of Christ, one baptism, one faith, one Lord Jesus, one Holy Spirit, and one God and Father of all, above all, through all, and living in all believers (Eph. 4:4-6).

It is reported that when the anointing was upon Evan

[29] Loc. cit.

Roberts, he spoke with great power and demonstration of the Spirit, urging the Christians to submit to and obey the will of God and to allow the Holy Spirit to break out in converting power upon the unsaved. One writer in Wales said at the time: "The Revival has brought us back to the Cross of Christ. Everywhere, the people throng in multitudes to hear this Holy Spirit-baptized young student speak. He spoke with 'impassioned oratory,' but once the overflowing stream had broken out, the Spirit of God appeared to put aside preaching and use the voice of testimony, proclaiming 'You slew him, hanging on a tree, Him did God exalt.' *This was the burden of the message, and the Holy Ghost bore witness by signs and wonders wrought amongst the thronging multitudes."*[30] (Italics supplied.)

Another account stated: "The glorious fact and outstanding feature of the mighty awakening was that the sense of the Lord's presence was everywhere throughout the entire nation. It bore the witness of thousands of young converts rejoicing in the thrill of their new-found Redeemer. *These were drunk with the new wine of the Spirit and like the young converts in the Book of Acts, they went everywhere preaching the Word, without the authority of man—having the ordination of the Holy Spirit."*[31] (Italics supplied.)

Mrs. Jessie Penn-Lewis has further written:

"The Spirit of God worked in mighty power in 'signs and wonders' being wrought among the people. 'Signs and wonders' in miracles of physical deliverance for souls. One convert who had been a gambler and a drunkard, with his bodily frame shattered by his life, gave testimony that since the day of his conversion, he had been perfectly restored to normal health.

"Others, too, told of the healing power of God. A minister tells how he was taken ill in the midst of his work, but he appealed to the Lord and found himself instantly healed."[32] As has been said, the Awakening in Wales was indeed "the Acts of the Apostles up-to-date. People fell to the ground under the conviction of the Holy Spirit. There were many

[30] *Ibid.*, p. 5
[31] *Loc. cit.*
[32] *Loc. cit.*

manifestations of the Holy Spirit. *There was tremendous singing, tremendous prayer—there was confession of sin and true repentance, and a complete coming out from the things of this world."* [33] As to the singing, one newspaper wrote: " 'The fact is, unless heard, it is unimaginable and when heard, it is indescribable.' No hymnbooks were used. Once a song was started, it seemed to be motivated by a simultaneous unity; the melody and song were caught up by the whole congregation, merging into a myriad-headed personality of song in a perfect blending of mood, purpose, and unity, which is only possible through the Spirit of God. Three-fourths of the meeting consisted of this 'singing in the Spirit.' 'It was a mighty chorus rising like the thunder of the surge on a rockbound shore.' " [34]

The beautiful harmonies and blending of voices in simultaneous unity without songbooks or leaders was visible and audible confirmation of community singing in the Spirit (i.e., in unknown tongues, not understood by the singers or hearers) mentioned by Paul in I Cor. 14:14-15. *This is more of that proclaimed by Joel and Peter.*

Group singing in unknown tongues in the Spirit is one of the miraculous signs and wonders being seen and heard with increasing frequency today among those in the Body of Christ who have received the baptism in the Holy Spirit. Having seen, heard, and participated many times since 1963 in such community singing in and led by the Spirit, I bear personal testimony as to the Holy authenticity, exquisite spontaneity, harmonious unity, and glorious wonder of it all. This singing of praises and worship to God defies verbal or written description. Only when one hears or participates in such singing can he appreciate the magnificence of God as He moves in this dimension by His Spirit! No wonder Paul exclaimed: "I will sing with the Spirit (that is, in languages I do not understand) and I will sing with the understanding also (that is, in my own daily language that I do understand)" (I Cor. 14:15). Paul sang in both dimensions—the natural and the supernatural. In I Tim. 1:16 and II Tim. 1:13 we are told that Paul is our pattern and we should hold fast to what he

[33] *Loc. cit.*
[34] *Ibid.*, p. 15.

has said. Again in Phil. 4:9 we are admonished to do the things that we have learned and heard that he did. He spoke and prayed and sang in his private devotions in tongues or languages he did not understand, more than all the Corinthian believers (I Cor. 14). Surely no true believer from Pentecost to this day could require any further direction or proof that it is God's purpose and will that the gifts of the Spirit accompanying the baptism are to be received and exercised as the Holy Spirit wishes and directs (I Cor. 12:11).

Other evidences of Pentecost in Wales were prayer meetings everywhere, reuniting of families and friends, a spirit of true unity, love and sacrifice in the Lord, prophesying under the control of the Holy Spirit, healings, payment of debts, and melting of hearts. Churches in Wales were filled to overflowing, and services were no longer formalistic but took their own course under the freedom and guidance of the Holy Spirit. A publication called the *Methodist Recorder* reported: *"the churches themselves have experienced a great quickening; and many, both ministers and people, have testified to a new joy and power and to receiving a Baptism in the Holy Spirit."*[35] (Italics supplied.) Thus in this revival was clearly seen the difference between the work of the Holy Spirit in conversion of the sinner, and the work of the Lord Jesus in baptizing the believer in the Holy Spirit—a distinction confirmed unmistakably by the Scriptures.

Some consider that the Welsh Revival was the greatest single spiritual revival of our century. It may well have been. But I would rather believe that it was but a part of the beginning in about 1900 of the greatest outpouring of the Holy Spirit in all history, which has continued steadily throughout the world for the past 70 years, with a tremendous unprecedented upsurge in the past 15 years. *This is all a part of that spoken of by Joel and Peter.*

Indonesia, 1966 to Date.

Most recent is the great revival in Indonesia in the past four years. This is a country of over 110 million people on about 10,000 islands, where 90% are Moslem, 6% Protestant, 3% Catholic and a small percentage Hindu, Buddhist, and

[35] *Loc. cit.*

Animist. When the communist coup failed in 1965, there was a natural and spiritual vacuum created. Into this vacuum the Spirit of God moved through a number of Christian believers. Hundreds of thousands have been converted to Christ. Countless numbers of believers have received the baptism in the Holy Spirit with all the apostolic signs and wonders following. This has included the manifestation of all nine of the gifts of the Spirit, including healings, deliverances, prayer meetings full of visible miraculous signs of the light and glow of God, speaking in tongues, prophecies, word of supernatural wisdom and knowledge, wholesale repentance and forsaking of crime, hunger for the Word of God, simple faith in and appropriating of the promises of God in the Scriptures, and at least 16 authenticated cases of raising of the dead. More recently it is reported that there have been others raised from the dead so there is no longer any exact count. Born-again Spirit-filled believers the world over have thrilled to hear and read about these accounts of the multitude of conversions to Christ and the miracle power of God in action in this fifth largest nation in the world. *This is the daily confirmation now happening in our midst of that proclaimed by the Holy Spirit through Joel and Peter.* [36]

[36] One of the best reports of the Indonesian revival is found in an article by John Myers, President of Voice Christian Publications, entitled: "Indonesia: the Greatest Work of God in the World Today," which appears in *Acts* magazine, Vol. I, No. 3, published in 1967, by Acts Publishers, P.O. Box 17066, Los Angeles, California 90017. This account of the great awakening sweeping Indonesia is based on stirring, firsthand reports from such reliable sources as: Mr. Ais Pormes, Baptist Minister and Indonesian Director for Campus Crusade for Christ; Dr. Clyde Taylor, General Director of N.A.E. (National Association of Evangelicals); and local missionaries and leaders of W.E.C. (Worldwide Evangelization Crusade).

Chapter IV

THE AWAKENING IS HERE

Paul said: "Awake, O sleeper, and arise from the dead, and Christ shall give you light" (Eph. 5:14).

The signs throughout the world today indicate we are in the beginning of such an awakening, renewal, and revival—the greatest of all time. And, praise God, this awakening is occurring in the historic established denominations, where the fresh breath of the wind of the Holy Spirit is blowing upon and bringing to life the dry bones. There never was a time when most of the visible church had more members *and less power.* Lukewarm and dry Christians are being stirred out of their complacency and sleep. Many are seeking because they are not being fed God's Word of Life from the pulpit. The Holy Spirit, more often than not through Spirit-filled laymen, is putting a hunger and thirst in their hearts for the reality and power of Jesus Christ. They are becoming dissatisfied with a ritual and form of godliness that either denies or knows nothing about the power thereof. The baptism in the Holy Spirit is the transforming answer to this need. Blessed are those who hunger and thirst after righteousness, for they shall be filled (Matt. 5:6). How else but with the Holy Spirit—the enduement of power from on high?

Those born-again Christians who have received this Pentecostal baptism are living and moving in a new and exciting dimension in the Holy Spirit. As part of the first fruits of this new life, God is establishing way stations in the homes of His children in all cities, towns, and villages throughout the world for the rest and shelter of His traveling ministers, evangelists, and prophets-at-large who are carrying the end-time message of the charismatic revival by the outpouring of the Holy Spirit in preparation for the soon coming of our Lord for His church. God is setting up a vast worldwide network of locations wherein laymen are finding a new and exciting dimension to proclaim Jesus Christ and His reality through study of the Word of God, prayer for the sick and help for the needy, and worship and praise of God. These ministries, which supplement the work of the organized churches, are found in private homes, offices of large and small corporations and other businesses, stores, farms, warehouses, restaurants, schools and universities, government buildings, assembly halls, mountain, forest, and oceanside camps, and open-air locations. There, by the charismatic work of the Holy Spirit, the Church is being awakened and the Gospel of Christ is reaching the lost.

For example, airline pilots of a major airline based on the east coast meet from time to time for Bible study and prayer and to tell other pilots and airline personnel about Jesus Christ. In the Los Angeles area, several groups of city and county employees meet regularly for prayer and Bible study and witnessing. These include some high officials and attorneys from city and county offices, among them attorneys from the district attorney's office. Similarly, there are several groups of employees at McDonnell Douglas Aircraft offices and facilities in Los Angeles County who regularly meet for the same purpose in Christ. In Hollywood there is a regular Christian fellowship of actors and others in the entertainment industry. In 1971, at the closing meeting of the Twenty-ninth Annual Convention of the National Association of Evangelicals in Los Angeles, California, Billy Graham remarked that he was amazed to discover in preparation for his last crusade in the spiritually hardened and resistant New York City area that there were about six thousand separate Christian prayer groups already existing and active, mostly in homes. These were made up of people from many denominations. The existence of most of them was known only to the immediate participants. Mr. Graham further remarked that we are witnessing today a return to the small home gatherings of the apostolic days of the first century—the church in the home (Acts 2:46).

Only God knows the number of small groups of born-again Christians who are gathering without fanfare but with fervent dedication and devotion all over the United States and the world in the name, faith, power, and authority of Jesus Christ for fellowship, prayer, worship, praise, and witness to carry out God's end-time plan.

While on a plane enroute from London to Edinburgh, Scotland, in October, 1966, I met and had delightful fellowship with an engineer who lived in a Midlothian town near Edinburgh. He was a former member of the Church of Scotland, but now he was a part of a small group of believers who banded together to meet regularly in homes for worship, Bible study, prayer, and praise led by the Holy Spirit. He emphasized again and again how the Holy Spirit guided them into greater and greater revelations of the reality of the person and lordship of Jesus Christ in all His fullness!

At the grass roots level God is raising up tens of thousands of such bands of believers against the worldwide flood of iniquity of the enemy (Isa. 5:18-23).

This work is being administered, not by any man or any man-made organization, but by the Holy Spirit Himself through His vast, fantastic, and unfathomable heavenly computer system. His omniscient and omnipotent computer would make our man-made missile and other systems seem like child's toys. He is leading and bringing together in the bond of complete unity and love and dynamic Spirit-led fellowship in Christ Jesus the individual talents of hundreds of thousands of born-again, blood-washed and Spirit-baptized sons and daughters of God. This is the real ecumenical movement in the world, directed by the Holy Spirit Himself— and not by ivory-towered world councils and conferences of churches. This is the true blending which will bring into operation the authority, power, love, fire, and boldness in the laymen to help complete and prepare the Body of Christ without spot, wrinkle, or blemish for the Bridegroom.

IT HAS BEEN SEEN AND HEARD

I have witnessed this ministry in action. God has used my law office as an "uttermost" place for people to learn about (and receive) Jesus Christ as Savior, to seek and receive the baptism in the Holy Spirit, as well as for prayer for healing of the sick, and prayer for other needs of clients. My waiting room has a supply of little Bibles, Gospels of John, and other Gospel literature for all visitors to read and take freely.

When clients, prospective clients, visiting attorneys, or friends pick up one of the booklets or inquire about them, the conversation is usually opened, and I am able to tell them about Jesus Christ.

A song urges us to expect a miracle every day, expect a miracle when we pray. As a relatively new Christian, I will verify that this can be literally true when we yield ourselves to God in faith and obedience and give Him a clear and open vessel through which His Holy Spirit may operate.

In my relatively short spiritual life, three persons who were about to commit suicide have called me. All were strangers to me. Through prayer with each, two on the telephone, God intervened and prevented tragedy.

One of these was a man of Jewish faith who had recently lost his lawyer wife. Because someone had told him I was a lawyer who had accepted Christ and might help him, he called me late one night, saying he had nothing to live for and intended to kill himself that night.

Under the leading of the Holy Spirit, I offered to drive to town and bring him to our home to stay overnight. He refused, but after we had prayed over the telephone, he promised God he would not take his life that night and agreed to see me in my office the next morning.

At nine o'clock in the morning he was there. Within an hour we were both on our knees in prayer. With tears in his eyes he repented of his sins and accepted Christ as his Savior.

One morning I gave my testimony for Christ in a city north of Los Angeles. That afternoon I visited with a client and his wife, both born-again Christians. She told me that the seventy-five-year-old father of one of her employees was critically ill with a kidney ailment. The doctors said he probably would not survive the night. The Lord impressed on our hearts that we should immediately visit the man and pray for him.

His children and other relatives were at first hesitant to admit us, thinking I was a minister. After we convinced them that I was only a lawyer who loved the Lord, they let us in.

The man was sitting half-propped-up in a chair to prevent his lungs from filling with fluid. I asked him if he believed Jesus could heal him. He answered with an affirmative nod. We laid our hands on him and, in the name of Jesus, asked God for deliverance and healing in body, mind, and soul. Then we persuaded the children and other relatives to join hands in a prayer circle, and again we prayed. The Lord's presence filled the room in a wonderful way.

That was the last time I ever saw the man. But I continued to pray for him when I returned home. God answered the prayers, and the old man survived the illness, to the amazement of all. Later I learned that his fear of death changed to a beautiful peace of mind he had never before known or displayed. He continually talked about how much God must love him to have sent strangers to pray for him. Now he knew Jesus Christ as Savior and was ready to meet Him whenever he called.

One day a former client in a central California city was hospitalized with a serious heart attack. He was not expected to live through the night. His wife called me from the hospital. I prayed with her for his recovery and deliverance. After we prayed, I received assurance from the Lord that he would survive and be a witness to others of God's great healing power. The woman returned to her husband's bedside and told the astonished nurse of the prayer on the telephone.

While the phone call was in progress, the patient had suddenly and dramatically improved. The nurse had witnessed immediate improvement in both breathing and color.

She reported the event to the doctors, who confirmed his improvement. As the Lord prophesied, my client quickly became a witness to others at the hospital of the power of God through Jesus Christ. Some days later the man left the hospital, fully recovered.

Not long afterward, a client came to my office for advice about a possible suit against certain county officials over disposition of a minor traffic ticket which carried a seventeen-dollar fine. In the confusion of a busy courtroom, the man had not been given an opportunity to get his money. He was thereupon sentenced to, and spent, three miserable days in the Los Angeles County jail. He was a respected business-man and a decorated combat hero in the Pacific in World War II.

The embarrassment of being treated as a common criminal and thrown in jail over a seventeen-dollar traffic fine, after the blood, sweat, and tears of his service for his country, became an obsession with him. It affected his whole life and relationships with his friends. He threatened to move his family to Australia.

After dissuading him from filing suit, I joined hands with him and his wife and prayed for his deliverance from his oppressive condition. The Lord answered the prayer, giving him a new peace of mind, love for Christ, and forgiveness for the officials who, he felt, had wronged him.

On another occasion, the seventy-four-year-old mother of a client was seriously ill in a Los Angeles hospital with a stroke which affected her speech and caused paralysis. I prayed for her on the telephone and in my office. God answered the prayer with a recovery that astonished her physicians. The client's sister telephoned me from Los Angeles to Phoenix, where I was attending a Christian Fellowship meeting, to report the recovery so I could share their joy at what the Lord had done for their mother.

The airliner, I have found, provides one of the most convenient environments for witnessing for Christ. The frank surprise of most people at hearing a lawyer talk about Jesus captures their interest and attention.

Once, on an eastbound plane, I was sitting alone praying that the Lord would send someone to whom I could witness. My large Bible was lying facedown on the adjoining seat. One of the stewardesses stopped beside it.

"Are you a minister?" she asked.

"No, I'm a lawyer," I replied.

"Oh," she said, "I thought that was a Bible, but I guess it's your lawbook."

"It's both," I explained.

She sat down and listened attentively while I told how my family and I had been saved at a Billy Graham crusade and had all been filled with the Holy Spirit. I shared with her the reality of a loving Heavenly Father who gives His children spiritual gifts so that they may serve Him more effectively. She was particularly interested in the gift which enables us to worship Him in heavenly languages.

She wanted to know more about the infilling of the Holy Spirit. Subsequently I sent her some Christian literature telling her of the present-day charismatic revival.

Like most lawyers in divorce matters, I have always attempted to see if reconciliation is possible before proceeding with the divorce. Since being converted and filled with the Spirit, I have a powerful new ally to help resolve marital difficulties in my office: prayer. I have prayed with divorce clients, individually and even together with the opposing spouse, with amazing results.

In one instance I spent most of one Saturday afternoon with a husband, a born-again Christian who had not been close to the Lord. We discussed his marital problems and prayed together in my office. Then we drove out to the Hollywood apartment of the couple to talk to his wife.

She proved to be a lovely Jewish Christian who loved the Lord. But there were a number of serious conflicts in their marriage, marked with bitterness, pride, accusations, and counteraccusations, and lack of understanding. For several hours that Saturday night they poured out their grievances against each other. As I counseled with them, advice sprinkled with Scripture I wasn't aware I knew came to mind.

Finally, we joined hands and prayed together, asking the Lord to restore the great love and joy that had existed in their marriage and to bring reconciliation.

The prayer was answered. I left them in each other's arms, happily reconciled.

Witnessing for Christ when the Holy Spirit leads has become a thrilling experience, wherever I am. This includes the halls of the Los Angeles County Courthouse.

Recently, in a trial court before a jury was called, we were discussing settlement of a personal injury case. While settlement negotiations were going on, I was enabled without strain or effort to reach ten persons with at least some of the Good News of Christ. These were my three clients, the wife of one of them, one of the opposing attorneys, the judge, the bailiff, the court clerk, the court reporter, and another attorney. The case was settled satisfactorily, all to the glory of the Lord!

God has given me a burden for my fellow attorneys and judges. I have told many of them about Jesus, and God's wondrous plan of salvation. With the help of the Lord, I hope to tell thousands more (there are over 10,000 in Los Angeles County alone) so that on Judgment Day they will not lose by default the most important case they ever handled on earth—the salvation of their own souls.

What is equally important in the eyes of the Lord, each attorney who is saved and filled with the Holy Spirit will, in his own sphere of influence, lead many other people to eternal life and glory through Jesus Christ.

Plainly, none of the incidents I have recounted is the result of my cleverness or personal ability, but each is a manifestation of the Holy Ghost at work. I am simply the earthen vessel, the ambassador for Christ; the excellency of the power is of God and not of me (II Cor. 4:7; 5:20).

I have heard personal testimonies of similar experiences in other law offices in Portland, Oregon, Forth Worth, Texas, and Atlanta, Georgia. I know a number of medical doctors, optometrists, and dentists and have read of many others throughout the country who preach Jesus in their offices and in hospitals, and who lay hands on the sick in Jesus' name. The same kind of faith is seen, too, among engineers, pilots, bankers, school teachers, college professors, actors, musicians, singers, and other professional and business men of a wide variety of callings. The Holy Spirit is moving vertically and horizontally throughout all levels of our society, from men in high places to the most humble laborers, to ignite them for Jesus Christ.

Recently a Christian engineer practicing in Los Angeles reported to me that he was led of the Spirit to attend a cocktail party. There he witnessed to the saving knowledge of Jesus Christ to a well-known actor who has played the role of a number of Bible characters in the movies but has apparently himself never known the reality of Him who is the Center of the Bible, Jesus Christ.

Now the cocktail party is not the orthodox place to preach the Gospel. But, praise the Lord, we have a God who is not bound by man's orthodoxy. Jesus sought and found the lost in the market-places. He sat down to eat with sinners. He took His wondrous Gospel to the people wherever they were or wherever they would congregate—in private homes, beside a well, from a ship at the lake's edge, on a mountainside. After Pentecost, the first members of the Body of Christ met and broke bread and worshiped in private homes and preached the Gospel everywhere.

RETURN TO THE PATTERN
OF THE EARLY CHURCH

Today we are witnessing a renewal and return to the original pattern laid down by our Lord in the early Church, sovereignly led and guided as always by the Holy Spirit, on a scale never known before in history. This certainly does not mean that God has forsaken such of the established denominational churches as are still preaching and teaching the pure and full Gospel of Christ and recognizing the charismatic work of the Holy Spirit in these last days. He will certainly confirm His word and use His people who worship Him in Spirit and in truth, wherever they are found, inside or outside the walls of a man-built church.

But God is assuredly bypassing, through this great awakening of laymen, every modern Laodicean-type church, lukewarm, self-satisfied, in need of nothing. Likewise He is bypassing any church where the Virgin Birth of Christ, efficacy of His precious Blood, His saving and redemptive work on the cross, His bodily Resurrection, His Ascension to Heaven, His soon physical return for His Church or any of such eternal truths are denied or neglected. He is bypassing any church where modernistic doctrines are preached which question the truth and validity of the Word of God or deny the existence, power, and operation of the charismatic gifts of the Holy Spirit. Also bypassed is any church composed of status-seeking members to whom the pure Gospel and Blood of Christ are either irrelevant or distasteful and where church architecture, sophistication, comfortable pews, and church social events are of prime importance rather than the saving of souls, the praising of God, healing of the sick, and deliverance of the oppressed.

THE WALK IN THE SPIRIT

But, praise His Holy name, God is not bypassing any born-again individuals in any of these churches who are spiritually hungering and thirsting and crying out for the true reality and life of Jesus Christ which can be found only in the enabling and revealing power of the Holy Spirit! These people are being baptized in and filled with the Holy Spirit and are leading transformed and dynamic lives in Christ with an exciting commitment more alive than anything in the secular world. Some are being delivered from the frustration and discouragement of trying to serve the Lord by their own efforts instead of allowing the Holy Spirit to do the work through them. Others are being delivered from the superficiality of shallow religious forms and rituals without the presence of the Holy Spirit. With this baptism and deliverance comes a new joy in the Lord Jesus that is truly full of glory. Also there comes a desire and freedom to praise and thank Him daily in and for all things, in our own native tongue and in the unknown language of the Holy Spirit. Moreover, we find a loving boldness to speak and proclaim His name and exercise the power to do His wonderful works without embarrassment as did the members of the First Century Church. Most important is the desire to become the instruments and temples through which the love of Christ by the power of the Holy Spirit will move as evangelist to save and deliver those who sit in darkness and in the shadow of death. Many moving in this dimension of the Holy Spirit will be empowered to minister as apostles, prophets, teachers, and pastors (according to the measure of the gift of Christ by grace). This will be for the purpose of perfecting and equipping the saints so that they in turn will be able to minister to and edify and build up the Church, which is the Body of Christ. Then we will see the fulfillment of Eph.

4:13, the becoming of one perfect composite man in the unity and oneness of the faith and knowledge of the Son of God, unto the measure of the stature of the fullness and completeness of Christ. Truly then we will become a part of that for which the whole creation has groaned and travailed and waited—the manifestation of the sons of God (Rom. 8:9-23).

PREPARATION FOR HIS SOON RETURN

Now what is the conclusion of the whole matter?

No one can deny that we are living in times unprecedented in history. There is an increasing and pyramiding of worldly knowledge in nuclear and other science and technology, without acknowledging God, that has fearful potential. People everywhere are calling out for peace, but wars, destruction, rebellion, oppression, violence, famine, and hatred continue. The Prince of Peace is the answer, but He is still rejected by the multitudes.

Iniquity and sin and lawlessness and unbelief abound today in a measure of defiant openness exceeding that of Sodom and Gomorrah. Darkness is thickening throughout the earth. All creation feels the pressure of the building up of all things to a soon climax of explosive events. Urgency is everywhere. No wonder that today we are beginning to see the hearts of many of the unsaved failing them with fear and for looking after those things which are soon coming on the earth (Luke 21:26). The world lives in an age of anxiety. Only the born-again believers who are flowing in the dimension of the Holy Spirit have no anxiety or fear, even with the possibility of going through some or all of the tribulation. On the contrary, these members of the Body of Christ are moving with joy and peace and anticipation in God's great end-of-the-age plan, being confident that where sin abounds, grace and mercy will much more abound before judgment.

Time is very short. The culminating judgments of this age are nearing fulfillment. It is apparent from the signs of the times that we are in the last days of that generation which shall not pass away until the fulfillment of those prophetic events mentioned in Luke 21, and Acts 2:19-20, for example, that will usher in the return of the Prince of Peace and a new age. Concurrently, already there has come, and will continue to come, a mighty outpouring of the Spirit of God in accordance with His revealed plan.

God's purpose for this period and age of grace and truth began with the manifestation on earth of Jesus Christ, His only begotten Son, the eternal Word of God made ·flesh, through whom is the gift of eternal life to all who in faith will believe and trust and love Him. This purpose was continued at Pentecost with the first great outpouring of the Holy Spirit, the promise of the Father, upon the 120. Jesus Christ was and is God's incomparable gift to the world. The Holy Spirit was and is Christ's supreme gift to His Church. What happened to those who received the gift of the Holy Spirit is recorded plainly in the Book of Acts. The miracles and healings performed by Jesus before Pentecost were continued in the first century after Pentecost by the power of His Holy Spirit moving through Peter, John, Stephen, Philip, Paul and the other faithful ones. The Book of Acts is set forth as a testimony, pattern, type, and example of what then followed and what has in fact followed down through the centuries, is now following, and will follow until the return of the Lord Jesus Christ.

We know now by irrefutable and trustworthy historical proof that what the early apostles received in the first century by the baptism in the Holy Spirit, has been received by countless true followers of Christ throughout the nineteen centuries' since Pentecost for the perpetuation of the Church in each generation and the fulfillment of God's plan for the church age. *We now know from history that the supernatural gifts were not invested just for the early church, but also for the Church throughout all generations until the Lord returns.*

The Holy Spirit is the administrator and executive officer of the Godhead for this church age. He is the flow of the mind and purpose of God the Father, carrying the reality of the Word of God, Christ Jesus, into the hearts of men, both sinners and believers. Without His indwelling, leading, and reign, Christian believers cannot carry out the eternal will and purpose of the Father. "For as many as are led by the Spirit of God, they are the sons of God" (Rom. 8:14). Without the Holy Spirit they cannot receive the fullness of all in all that has been given by the Father to the Son. It is the Holy Spirit Who enables born-again Christians to live victorious lives! Without the Holy Spirit they cannot exercise the gifts of the Spirit nor produce the fruit of the Spirit. Without the fullness of the Holy Spirit they will not be able to stand against the enemy in the perilous and darkening times in which we live, nor in the greater tribulation to come. They will be without the needed edification of direct and personal communication with our Heavenly Father in a new and heavenly tongue (I Cor. 14:2 ff).

No true believer should be fearful of the gift of praying in tongues. It is the private line of communication between us and our Heavenly Father (I Cor. 14:2). It is the overflowing of the Holy Spirit that pours out to bless those around us. The natural man does not understand this supernatural phenomenon. Nor can he, because it is of the Holy Spirit who does not live in the unregenerated man. But the believer who has already been sealed with the earnest of the Holy Spirit is without excuse to deny the very fullness of this same Holy Spirit, and thus also without excuse to deny speaking in tongues, prophesying, healing the sick and brokenhearted, casting out demons, and the other signs and wonders following (Mark 16:15-20).

These supernatural manifestations are needed today as never before to demonstrate to a materialistic, mechanized, scientific, unbelieving world the eternal power and wisdom of God. We dare not limit God. For the days are upon us when nothing will avail to break through the overwhelming power of the enemy except the supernatural power of God which most of the visible church today knows very little about.

THIS IS THAT

The baptism in the Holy Spirit is available now, today, to all flesh, all mankind who believe, trust, and have faith in Jesus Christ. The Lord Jesus, the Baptizer, is now pouring out of the Holy Spirit as never before since Pentecost. The evidence is overwhelming that we are in the midst of the last great outpouring before the return of the Lord Jesus Christ! It is vital now that all believers who hunger and thirst for more of the fullness of God come quickly to the knowledge of this truth before it is too late. Let them in love and obedience and faith seek the baptism in the Holy Spirit. "How much more shall your Heavenly Father give the Holy Spirit to them that ask?" (Luke 11:13). It is the promise of the Father (Acts 1:4). Having received this promise when He was exalted at the right hand of the Father, the Lord Jesus Christ is shedding forth this holy gift to all who believe and ask (Acts 2:38-39).

With the baptism will come the power and authority and love and fire and boldness to do the will and accomplish the purpose of the Father in these last hours to prepare the way for the very soon return of the Lord. What an exciting, thrilling challenge and prospect it is to all who expectantly wait and watch for His return!

Praise His Holy name forever!

PSEU-DO CHRISTIANS by Dr. Ray Jarman A516/1.00
The dangers of liberal and occult
teaching in lives of Christians and non-Christians.
Dr. Jarman for 50 years was a leader in science of the mind
religions until a dramatic conversion at 70 years of age.

THIS EARTH'S END by Carmen Benson A513/95¢
The Bible contains prophecy telling how this earth
will end. This is a clearly written, easy to understand
explanation of dreams and visions in the New Testament.

JESUS AND ISRAEL by Carmen Benson A514/95¢
The Old Testament revealed through dreams and visions
the future happenings on the earth. An accurate account
of things to come.

WALK IN THE SPIRIT by Michael Harper L319/95¢
Renewal or Revolution — The Church must decide. Some have
discovered a new dimension in living through God's power.

GONE IS SHADOW'S CHILD by Jessie Foy L337/95¢
A moving story of a mother's faith in God for
her son and of a highly effective B10-chemical
treatment called megavitamin in schizophrenia.

SPIRITUAL WARFARE A505/95¢
A practical study on demon oppression and exorcism.
A positive method in freeing the oppressed.

GOD'S JUNKIE by Sonnie Arguinzoni
with Jouinn Ricketts A509/95¢
Introduction by David Wilkerson
A former junkie (his story is in Run Baby Run)
tells of the unique addict church — "Miracles do
happen" by Nicky Cruz.

NINE O'CLOCK IN THE MORNING by Dennis Bennett
Introduction by John Sherrill. A511/95¢
After 7 big print-ups in hardcover. An Episcopal
Rector, Dennis Bennett was the center of the
religious new events 10 years ago because of the
"Speaking in Tongues" experience.

HEAR MY CONFESSION by Fr. Joseph E. Orsini
L341/95¢ A Roman Catholic priest tells his
personal story of how he discovered the CAtholic
Pentecostal experience.

RUN BABY RUN by Nicky Cruz L-101/95¢
The true story of a gang leader turned crusader.

THE LONELY NOW by Nicky Cruz
with Jamie Buckingham A510/95¢
Nicky answers the questions youth ask.

THE CHALLENGING COUNTERFEIT
by Raphael Gasson L102/95¢
Hidden secrets of spiritualism disclosed by a former medium who tells
how to know the real.

ANGELS OF LIGHT? by Dr. Hobart Freeman A506/95¢
Dr. Freeman reveals the source of power in the popular occult practices
and the deliverance from them.

EMOTIONAL ILLS AND THE CHRISTIAN
by G.J. Guldseth, M.D. A507/95¢
A high percentage of illness is attributed to the psychosomatic.
Dr. Guldseth discusses ways of healing through the Bible.

PRISON TO PRAISE
by Chaplain (LTC) M. Carothers A504/95¢
Revolutionary concepts in achieving remarkable answers to
problems through praise.

THE SPIRIT BADE ME GO
by David du Plessis L-325/95¢
A charismatic journey of one man bringing him before thousands in a
world-wide ecumenical mission for the Holy Spirit.

WISE UP! HOW? by Clinton White L-318/95¢
"I was an alcoholic fourteen years and addicted to drugs. I was set
free. I call it a miracle."
